Nonprofit Finance:
A Practical Guide

Second Edition

Sheila Shanker, CPA

Published by Create Space- Sheila Shanker – U.S.A. 2017

Cover by Debora K. Lewis

ISBN-13:978-1975996581
ISBN-10:1975996585

To my children, Yohan and Yasmin Shanker

CONTENTS

1- Introduction

T his book provides a detailed overview of the major nonprofit areas for persons interested in the financial operations of an organization, such as financial statements, accounting, grant management, internal controls and tax issues.

I recommend this publication as a useful, practical resource for any new controller, manager, board member, or CFO working in the nonprofit sector. Maybe you have questions regarding operations or specific accounting issues, such as:

- Is the nonprofit tax-exempt?
- What are "funds" or "net assets"?
- What is a "release of net assets"?
- What is a Statement of Position?
- What is a Statement of Activities?

This book answers these questions and others you may have in the back of your mind regarding the nonprofit sector. Some chapters are more technical than others are, so if you're not accounting-oriented, you may still understand the concepts as terms and vocabulary are explained with numerous examples to clarify typical nonprofit models of operation, taxes, and financial reporting.

Samples of letters, forms, and reports pertinent to the nonprofit world are presented along with vignettes of my own experiences and recommendations, giving this material a different perspective from a purely academic or technical approach.

Each chapter covers an important topic within the nonprofit world, combining theory and practical information to make the issues clear and straightforward to understand.

Upcoming changes to financial statements are covered here including significant aspects of FASB ASU 2016-14 *Presentation of Financial Statements of Not-for-Profit Entities*. We also review ASU 2014-09 *Revenue from Contracts with Customers* and ASU 2016-02 *Leases*.

The publication is based on the IRS, Financial Accounting Standards Board (FASB), and other government publications, including the "Super Circular," a federal grant guide. Please note that, like everything in life, things change, and you must keep up with the updates in the law and accounting regulations that come along, not yet picked up by this publication.

I hope you find this book an informative and valuable resource to better understand and appreciate the nonprofit sector.

2 - Nonprofit Basics

"Wikipedia is a non-profit. It was either the dumbest thing I ever did or the smartest thing I ever did. Communities can build amazing things, but you have to be part of that community, and you cannot abuse them. You have to be very respectful of what their needs are."

Jimmy Wales, founder of Wikipedia (Keynote Speech, SXSW 2006)

W ikipedia is indeed one of the thousands of nonprofits based in the United States providing goods and services to many communities for decades. The nonprofit sector isn't just a new fad, as the U.S. has a long history of philanthropy.

One of the first organized campaigns for donations was the "United Thank Offering," created by the Episcopal Church in 1889. Christmas Seals was founded in the early 1900s due to the spread of tuberculosis and other lung diseases. Other known charities, such as the Boy Scouts, National Association for the Advancement of Colored People, and Goodwill, were created between 1909 and 1913.

The nonprofit sector is growing, with about 962,000 public charities in the U.S. in 2014. Such organizations were also responsible for 9.2% of all salaries paid in the U.S. in 2010, according to the National Center for Charitable Statistics.

The largest nonprofit organization is the Bill and Melinda Gates Foundation, with an endowment of about $40.3 billion, including billions donated by Warren Buffet.

Characteristics of Nonprofits

Many people think that nonprofits are parts of government entities. That's not correct. Nonprofits are separate organizations that may or may not receive money from governments. They are also known as "charities," "exempt organizations," or "NPOs," and can be large or small. Several prominent hospitals and universities like Kaiser Permanente and UCLA are set up as nonprofits. Other well-known nonprofits are the Better Business Bureau, Carnegie Corporation of New York, and the New York State Society of CPAs.

Outside the U.S., the United Kingdom recognizes nonprofits as "charities" that must be registered with the U.K. Charity Commission. Some countries call nonprofits "NGOs," nongovernmental organizations. The idea is the same—these entities aren't governmental, but receive funding from governments and other entities to conduct tasks relevant to their missions.

Nonprofits have some essential characteristics that make operating and managing their finances different from the for-profit business. Some of these features are:

- No profit motive

- No ownership

- o Different revenue streams

- o Volunteers

No Profit Motive

As the name suggests, nonprofit organizations aren't interested in profits. Their reason for conducting business is to help an individual community, serve a public interest. So, while they need enough money to pay their bills, the focus is on programs, mission statements, not on sale revenues.

Due to this crucial difference, the culture and management of a nonprofit are often different from other sectors. For example, employees or volunteers may be more passionate about the work, and emotions may run higher in this environment as compared to regular businesses.

As expected, you'll not see the word "profit" when reviewing financial statements of nonprofits. In fact, nonprofit accounting and finance have their own vocabulary and concepts that are a bit different from the for-profit world.

No Ownership

Nonprofit organizations have the unique status of possessing no "real" ownership. They retain boards of directors, but not owners per se. The idea is that nonprofits are actually "owned" by a community or members they serve. Also, such organizations can't be sold as other businesses can.

✓ **A nonprofit organization is a business unable to hold or distribute profits.**

These entities can't distribute earnings, issue, or sell stocks. As expected, since nonprofits can't pay dividends on any earnings, and have no owners, people can't "invest" in these organizations the same way that they can in a regular business. A person or firm can promote individual programs by donating to a nonprofit, but the expectation of getting a return on investment doesn't exist.

In the nonprofit work, the mission statement is the primary focus for operations. If the mission is to provide shoes to homeless kids, for example, all activities should be concentrated to this end, not to sell shoes for a profit.

Different Revenue Streams

Income sources of nonprofits are different from those of for-profits that obtain their funds from goods and services sold at a profit. Nonprofit revenues typically come from fundraising events and:

- Governments
- Foundations
- Businesses
- Individual donors
- Trusts
- Estates

Organizations may receive money for various purposes depending on their mission statements. Some conduct or support medical research, and receive funds from government, such as NIH (National Institutes of Health), family trusts, or foundations interested in specific illnesses. Such grants and gifts have different compliance issues, making this area quite challenging to manage.

Nonprofits often mention generous donors or "patrons" on their literature and brochures, providing supporters with visibility and goodwill. The idea is to engage the community to value the goods and services, and donate to special events and campaigns.

✓ **You can quickly recognize a nonprofit website by the ".org" at the end of the website address although colleges may have ".edu" at the end of the address.**

Volunteers

Since funding is limited in many organizations, volunteering is a vital characteristic of nonprofits. People volunteer for all kinds of jobs, from administrative assistants to presidents. Also, many businesses offer their employees to volunteer as a contribution to the community. In fact, some organizations run on volunteers alone. Managing these unpaid workers can be challenging, but done right, it can greatly benefit the programs and the community.

As controller of a nonprofit, I had an interesting experience with a volunteer. A developmentally disabled woman used to help with Accounts Payable filing. She was a valuable member of the department and felt good about having something important to do. The Accounts Payable accountant was happy to receive the assistance, making this a win-win situation So, volunteers can be a big help when appropriately managed.

Tax-Exempt Status

In the U.S., a nonprofit organization is a business entity that has received an exemption from the IRS, so it doesn't pay income taxes as other firms do. However, many nonprofits are required to file reports about their activities, even though they may not pay anything.

Nonprofits or tax-exempt organizations come in a variety of code sections related to the nature of the entity. For example, chambers of commerce can become tax-exempt under Section 501(c)(6), not 501(c)(3). Following is a list of the code sections related to tax-exemption options.

501(c)(1)	Corporations created by Congress, such as Federal Credit Unions
501(c)(2)	Title-holding corporations for exempt organizations. Limited to own real estate and collect funds
501(c)(3)	**Nonprofit, religious, and educational organizations, including many hospitals. The 501(c)(3) is the focus of this publication.**
501(c)(4)	Various political education organizations
501(c)(5)	Labor unions and agriculture
501(c)(6)	Business league and chamber of commerce organizations
501(c)(7)	Recreational club organizations
501(c)(8)	Fraternal beneficiary societies
501(c)(9)	Voluntary employee beneficiary associations
501(c)(10)	Fraternal lodge societies
501(c)(11)	Teachers' retirement fund associations
501(c)(12)	Local benevolent life insurance associations, mutual irrigation, telephone companies, and like organizations
501(c)(13)	Cemetery companies
501(c)(14)	Credit unions
501(c)(15)	Mutual insurance companies
501(c)(16)	Corporations organized to finance crop operations
501(c)(17)	Employees' associations
501(c)(18)	Employee-funded pension trusts created before June 25, 1959
501(c)(19)	Veterans' organizations
501(c)(20)	Group legal services plan organizations
501(c)(21)	Black lung benefit trusts
501(c)(22)	Withdrawal liability payment fund
501(c)(23)	Veterans' organizations created before 1880
501(c)(24)	Section 4049 ERISA Trusts
501(c)(25)	Title-holding corporations for qualified exempt organizations
501(c)(26)	State-sponsored high-risk health coverage organizations
501(c)(27)	State-sponsored workers' compensation reinsurance organizations
501(c)(28)	National railroad retirement investment trust

All entities mentioned are tax-exempt for different reasons. A chamber of commerce, for instance, is formed to support local businesses, while a food bank is created to help the poor. These entities are tax-exempt, even if they differ in mission and objectives.

The focus of this publication relates to organizations that are tax-exempt under 501(c)(3). Whenever a "nonprofit" or "nonprofit organization" is mentioned, assume we are dealing with a 501(c)(3) organization. Section 501(c)(3) lists the following exempt purposes:

- Charitable
- Educational
- Religious
- Scientific
- Literary
- Public safety testing
- Cruelty prevention to children and animals
- Support of sports competitions

The IRS keeps an "Exempt Organizations Business Master File" that identifies nonprofits exempted under 501(c)(3) and other sections. Many grantors will only accept grant applications from organizations on this list.

Form 1023

A corporation submits this form to the IRS to become an exempt organization under Section 501(c)(3). This crucial process is usually done within twenty-seven months of the corporation creation.

When the organization files Form 1023 within the prescribed time, the tax exemption is valid from the date of incorporation. If it files Form 1023 after twenty-seven months of incorporation, the tax exemption is likely to start from the filing date forward.

Depending on the size of the organization, Form 1023-EZ, a streamlined version of the form 1023 can be used and filed electronically. However, the eligibility worksheet on the instructions for 1023-EZ must be filled out first to be sure the organization meets all the requirements. The worksheet requests information on the size of the organization, assets, income, and types of activities. A sample 1023-EZ form follows.

Form **1023-EZ**

(June 2014)

Department of the Treasury
Internal Revenue Service

Streamlined Application for Recognition of Exemption
Under Section 501(c)(3) of the Internal Revenue Code

▸ Do not enter social security numbers on this form as it may be made public.
▸ Information about Form 1023-EZ and its separate instructions is at *www.irs.gov/form1023*.

OMB No. 1545-0056

Note: *If exempt status is approved, this application will be open for public inspection.*

☐ Check this box to attest that you have completed the Form 1023-EZ Eligibility Worksheet in the current instructions, are eligible to apply for exemption using Form 1023-EZ, and have read and understand the requirements to be exempt under section 501(c)(3).

Part I   Identification of Applicant

1a Full Name of Organization

b Address (number, street, and room/suite). If a P.O. box, see instructions.	**c** City		**d** State	**e** Zip Code + 4

2 Employer Identification Number	**3** Month Tax Year Ends (MM)	**4** Person to Contact if More Information is Needed

5 Contact Telephone Number	**6** Fax Number (optional)	**7** User Fee Submitted

8 List the names, titles, and mailing addresses of your officers, directors, and/or trustees. (If you have more than five, see instructions.)

First Name:	Last Name:		Title:	
Street Address:	City:	State:		Zip Code + 4:
First Name:	Last Name:		Title:	
Street Address:	City:	State:		Zip Code + 4:
First Name:	Last Name:		Title:	
Street Address:	City:	State:		Zip Code + 4:
First Name:	Last Name:		Title:	
Street Address:	City:	State:		Zip Code + 4:
First Name:	Last Name:		Title:	
Street Address:	City:	State:		Zip Code + 4:

9 a Organization's Website (if available):

b Organization's Email (optional):

Part II   Organizational Structure

1 To file this form, you must be a corporation, an unincorporated association, or a trust. **Check the box** for the type of organization.
☐ Corporation   ☐ Unincorporated association   ☐ Trust

2 ☐ **Check this box** to attest that you have the organizing document necessary for the organizational structure indicated above.
(See the instructions for an explanation of **necessary organizing documents**.)

3 Date incorporated if a corporation, or formed if other than a corporation (MMDDYYYY):

4 State of incorporation or other formation:

5 Section 501(c)(3) requires that your organizing document must limit your purposes to one or more exempt purposes within section 501(c)(3).
☐ **Check this box** to attest that your organizing document contains this limitation.

6 Section 501(c)(3) requires that your organizing document must not expressly empower you to engage, otherwise than as an insubstantial part of your activities, in activities that in themselves are not in furtherance of one or more exempt purposes.
☐ **Check this box** to attest that your organizing document does not expressly empower you to engage, otherwise than as an insubstantial part of your activities, in activities that in themselves are not in furtherance of one or more exempt purposes.

7 Section 501(c)(3) requires that your organizing document must provide that upon dissolution, your remaining assets be used exclusively for section 501(c)(3) exempt purposes. Depending on your entity type and the state in which you are formed, this requirement may be satisfied by operation of state law.
☐ **Check this box** to attest that your organizing document contains the dissolution provision required under section 501(c)(3) or that you do not need an express dissolution provision in your organizing document because you rely on the operation of state law in the state in which you are formed for your dissolution provision.

For Paperwork Reduction Act Notice, see the instructions.   Catalog No. 66267N   Form **1023-EZ** (6-2014)

Form 1023-EZ (6-2014)   Page **2**

Part III   Your Specific Activities

1   Enter the appropriate 3-character NTEE Code that best describes your activities (See the instructions): _____

2   To qualify for exemption as a section 501(c)(3) organization, you must be organized and operated exclusively to further one or more of the following purposes. By checking the box or boxes below, you attest that you are organized and operated exclusively to further the purposes indicated. **Check all that apply.**

☐ Charitable   ☐ Religious   ☐ Educational
☐ Scientific   ☐ Literary   ☐ Testing for public safety
☐ To foster national or international amateur sports competition   ☐ Prevention of cruelty to children or animals

3   To qualify for exemption as a section 501(c)(3) organization, you must:
   • Refrain from supporting or opposing candidates in political campaigns in any way.
   • Ensure that your net earnings do not inure in whole or in part to the benefit of private shareholders or individuals (that is, board members, officers, key management employees, or other insiders).
   • Not further non-exempt purposes (such as purposes that benefit private interests) more than insubstantially.
   • Not be organized or operated for the primary purpose of conducting a trade or business that is not related to your exempt purpose(s).
   • Not devote more than an insubstantial part of your activities attempting to influence legislation or, if you make a section 501(h) election, not normally make expenditures in excess of expenditure limitations outlined in section 501(h).
   • Not provide commercial-type insurance as a substantial part of your activities.
   ☐ **Check this box** to attest that you have not conducted and will not conduct activities that violate these prohibitions and restrictions.

4   Do you or will you attempt to influence legislation? . . . .   ☐ Yes ☐ No
   (If yes, consider filing Form 5768. See the instructions for more details.)

5   Do you or will you pay compensation to any of your officers, directors, or trustees? . . . .   ☐ Yes ☐ No
   (Refer to the instructions for a definition of **compensation**.)

6   Do you or will you donate funds to or pay expenses for individual(s)? . . . .   ☐ Yes ☐ No

7   Do you or will you conduct activities or provide grants or other assistance to individual(s) or organization(s) outside the United States? . . . .   ☐ Yes ☐ No

8   Do you or will you engage in financial transactions (for example, loans, payments, rents, etc.) with any of your officers, directors, or trustees, or any entities they own or control? . . . .   ☐ Yes ☐ No

9   Do you or will you have unrelated business gross income of $1,000 or more during a tax year? . . . . .   ☐ Yes ☐ No

10 Do you or will you operate bingo or other gaming activities? . . . .   ☐ Yes ☐ No

11 Do you or will you provide disaster relief? . . . .   ☐ Yes ☐ No

Part IV   Foundation Classification

Part IV is designed to classify you as an organization that is either a private foundation or a public charity. Public charity status is a more favorable tax status than private foundation status.

1   If you qualify for public charity status, check the appropriate box (**1a – 1c** below) and skip to **Part V** below.

   a ☐ **Check this box** to attest that you normally receive at least one-third of your support from public sources or you normally receive at least 10 percent of your support from public sources, and you have other characteristics of a publicly supported organization. **Sections 509(a)(1) and 170(b)(1)(A)(vi)**.

   b ☐ **Check this box** to attest that you normally receive more than one-third of your support from a combination of gifts, grants, contributions, membership fees, and gross receipts (from permitted sources) from activities related to your exempt functions and normally receive not more than one-third of your support from investment income and unrelated business taxable income. **Section 509(a)(2)**.

   c ☐ **Check this box** to attest that you are operated for the benefit of a college or university that is owned or operated by a governmental unit. **Sections 509(a)(1) and 170(b)(1)(A)(iv)**.

2   If you are not described in item 1a – 1c above, you are a private foundation. As a private foundation, you are required by section 508(e) to have specific provisions in your organizing document, unless you rely on the operation of state law in the state in which you were formed to meet these requirements. These specific provisions require that you operate to avoid liability for private foundation excise taxes under sections 4941-4945.

   ☐ **Check this box** to attest that your organizing document contains the provisions required by section 508(e) or that your organizing document does not need to include the provisions required by section 508(e) because you rely on the operation of state law in your particular state to meet the requirements of section 508(e). (See the instructions for explanation of the section 508(e) requirements.)

Form **1023-EZ** (6-2014)

18

Form 1023-EZ (6-2014) — — — — — — — — Page **3**

Part V Reinstatement After Automatic Revocation

Complete this section only if you are applying for reinstatement of exemption after being automatically revoked for failure to file required annual returns or notices for three consecutive years, and you are applying for reinstatement under section 4 or 7 of Revenue Procedure 2014-11. (Check only one box.)

1 ☐ **Check this box** if you are seeking retroactive reinstatement under section 4 of Revenue Procedure 2014-11. By checking this box, you attest that you meet the specified requirements of section 4, that your failure to file was not intentional, and that you have put in place procedures to file required returns or notices in the future. (See the instructions for requirements.)

2 ☐ **Check this box** if you are seeking reinstatement under section 7 of Revenue Procedure 2014-11, effective the date you are filing this application.

Part VI Signature

☐ I declare under the penalties of perjury that I am authorized to sign this application on behalf of the above organization and that I have examined this application, and to the best of my knowledge it is true, correct, and complete.

PLEASE
SIGN
HERE

(Type name of signer)

(Type title or authority of signer)

(Signature of Officer, Director, Trustee, or other authorized official)

Form **1023-EZ** (6-2014)

Form 1023-EZ is filed electronically only on Pay.gov.

19

The amounts payable with the Form 1023 vary with the size of the organization. The regular fee is $850. However, nonprofits that have or expect to have no more than $40,000 in gross revenue for the first four years combined pay a fee of $400.

If qualified for the 1023-EZ, smaller organizations pay only $275. Double check on the fee since it has changed over the years and is likely to change again. Nonprofits' staff should attach Form 8718 to the payment.

As they wait for the form 1023 to be approved, most organizations operate as tax-exempt and file nonprofit tax returns. Entities can follow the approval status on the IRS website.

Note that churches don't typically need to file 1023—the IRS gives them tax exemption automatically. However, many choose to submit the Form 1023 to affirm their status to donors and others.

Determination Letter

The IRS "Determination" letter is the "holy grail," as it's the proof that the organization is indeed tax-exempt and can receive tax-deductible donations. Management should keep its determination letter in a safe place, make copies of it and keep them secure because many funders and grantors require the letter in their application process.

In the past, the IRS would issue an Advance Ruling letter before its Final Determination letter. Later, the IRS streamlined this process for 501(c)(3) organizations, mailing a determination letter upon approval of the nonprofit. There is no need to file Form 8734 anymore. If management loses the original document, the IRS sends out "Affirmation" letters, confirming the tax-exempt status.

Note that the IRS may revoke 501(c)(3) tax-exempt status for various reasons, such as the failure to file tax returns for three consecutive years or excessive lobbying activities. Organizations may promote legislation up to a certain point but can't participate in political activity, including endorsing candidates for public office.

Sometimes the IRS makes mistakes and nonprofits lose their tax exemption, so be sure to look at the IRS Master Database often. If your problems aren't resolved promptly, contact the IRS Taxpayer Assistance Program.

Some businesses and foundations offer online gran

t applications that match the nonprofit's employer Identification number to the IRS master database. If the numbers don't match, the organization can't apply for assistance online or otherwlse. Therefore, it's essential to ensure the information in the Master Database is correct and routlnely updated. Go to the IRS website www.irs.gov to check it out.

Note that individual states, counties, and cities have different compliance requirements for nonprofits. For example, in California, organizations' founders must file Form 3500A, "Submission of Exemption Request," after receiving the tax exemption from the IRS.

Samples of IRS determination and affirmation letters are presented next.

Sheila Shanker

Determination letter

INTERNAL REVENUE SERVICE
P. O. BOX 2508
CINCINNATI, OH 45201

Date: **MAR 3 0 2007**

DEPARTMENT OF THE TREASURY

Employer Identification Number:

DLN:

Contact Person:
TE# .
Contact Telephone Number:

Accounting Period Ending:
June 30
Public Charity Status:
170(b)(1)(A)(vi)
Form 990 Required:
Yes
Effective Date of Exemption:
January 24, 2007
Contribution Deductibility:
Yes
Advance Ruling Ending Date:
June 30, 2011

Dear Applicant:

We are pleased to inform you that upon review of your application for tax exempt status we have determined that you are exempt from Federal income tax under section 501(c)(3) of the Internal Revenue Code. Contributions to you are deductible under section 170 of the Code. You are also qualified to receive tax deductible bequests, devises, transfers or gifts under section 2055, 2106 or 2522 of the Code. Because this letter could help resolve any questions regarding your exempt status, you should keep it in your permanent records.

Organizations exempt under section 501(c)(3) of the Code are further classified as either public charities or private foundations. During your advance ruling period, you will be treated as a public charity. Your advance ruling period begins with the effective date of your exemption and ends with advance ruling ending date shown in the heading of the letter.

Shortly before the end of your advance ruling period, we will send you Form 8734, Support Schedule for Advance Ruling Period. You will have 90 days after the end of your advance ruling period to return the completed form. We will then notify you, in writing, about your public charity status.

Please see enclosed Information for Exempt Organizations Under Section 501(c)(3) for some helpful information about your responsibilities as an exempt organization.

Letter 1045 (DO/CG)

-2-

Sincerely,

Enclosures: Information for Organizations Exempt Under Section 501(c)(3)
Statute Extension

Letter 1045 (DO/CG)

Sheila Shanker

Affirmation letter

IRS Department of the Treasury
Internal Revenue Service

P.O. Box 2508
Cincinnati OH   45201

In reply refer to:
Sep. 27, 2010 LTR 4168C EO

00015111
BODC: TE

Employer Identification Number:
Person to Contact:
Toll Free Telephone Number:

Dear Taxpayer:

This is in response to your Sep. 16, 2010, request for information regarding your tax-exempt status.

Our records indicate that you were recognized as exempt under section 501(c)(3) of the Internal Revenue Code in a determination letter issued in March 1995.

Our records also indicate that you are not a private foundation within the meaning of section 509(a) of the Code because you are described in section(s) 509(a)(1) and 170(b)(1)(A)(vi).

Donors may deduct contributions to you as provided in section 170 of the Code. Bequests, legacies, devises, transfers, or gifts to you or for your use are deductible for Federal estate and gift tax purposes if they meet the applicable provisions of sections 2055, 2106, and 2522 of the Code.

Please refer to our website www.irs.gov/eo for information regarding filing requirements. Specifically, section 6033(j) of the Code provides that failure to file an annual information return for three consecutive years results in revocation of tax-exempt status as of the filing due date of the third return for organizations required to file.

If you have any questions, please call us at the telephone number shown in the heading of this letter.

Sincerely yours,

24

Summary

Nonprofits are a growing sector of the U.S. economy that can't be ignored as they provide valuable goods and services to many communities, such as shelters for the homeless. The nonprofits focused in this publication are the ones tax-exempt under 501(c)(3), such as charities and social services organizations. These organizations may receive government grants and have dedicated volunteers who must be managed appropriately.

The IRS is the federal entity that approves and maintains tax exemptions, although states may mandate their particular requirements as well. The IRS determination and affirmation letters are evidence of an organization's tax-exempt status. Additionally, the IRS keeps a "Master Database" of tax-exempt organizations for public information on its website.

3 - Structure of Nonprofits

"Men love to organize."

James Mooney, U.S. business executive (1884-1957)

N onprofits and for-profit organizations can look the same on the surface, as both offer goods and services, collect money, provide classes, pay bills,   etc., but there's one main difference:

✓ **Nonprofits aren't interested in making a profit.**

The nonprofit's goal is to provide a public service, not to enrich owners. Ownership doesn't even exist in the nonprofit world. Such organizations don't issue stocks or dividends; they're not part of the stock market. Their financial statements don't present "Owner's Equity" or "Stockholder Equity" sections.

However, someone does "mind the store." Many people—stakeholders—are often involved in the daily operation and success of the organization.

Some typical stakeholders of a nonprofit organization are:

- Board of Directors
- Donors
- Grantors
- Banks
- Volunteers
- Community

Besides these "watchers," the founders often actively participate as members of the board of directors, helping with funding and program leadership. These passionate individuals have a lot of emotional attachment to the nonprofit, providing a vision for management and the community.

A vision is important, but the organization should also have a structure to ensure smooth operations and proper delivery of services. To this end, many nonprofits employ a president, vice-presidents, finance manager, and others, to supervise different sections. As with any business, size matters, and many large organizations are set up into "chapters" reporting to a headquarter office.

The board of directors and other jobs can be filled by volunteers, including the role of president. Many nonprofits are run entirely by volunteers.

All sections of an organization must work well together to fulfill the nonprofit's mission efficiently..

Also, grantors often require certain minimum management standards, making it essential for nonprofits to implement controls and reliable reporting mechanisms to be viable. It's not any surprise that some universities offer programs in nonprofit management and leadership, highlighting the specific needs of this sector. Actually, the Nonprofit Academic Centers Council (NACC) voted at its annual meeting in 2017 to start an accreditation process for its higher education members.

Operational Areas

Any business needs a structure to operate efficiently, and nonprofits are no different. Similar to for-profits, nonprofits work with a method and within a budget, as they must demonstrate positive outcomes to donors, board members, and the government.

Any business must have an effective framework to keep things running smoothly. This situation is especially true in the nonprofit sector where operations support the organization in many functional sections, including:

- Office management
- Program management
- Accounting and finance
- Administration
- Human resources
- Information technology
- Marketing and development

These functions, reflecting operations, can be classified into three areas, all supervised by the board of directors:

- Programs/Services
- Management and General
- Fundraising

The "top boss" is the board of directors. Many organizations retain executive directors who report to the board, while all departments report to this director. Below is a typical organizational chart of a nonprofit:

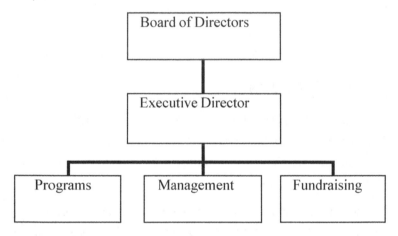

Identification of the three main areas of nonprofit operations (programs, management, and fundraising) is crucial to establish appropriate accounting systems, internal controls, reporting, and management.

Nonprofits' tax returns and financial statements are organized in three areas: programs, administration, and fundraising.

An issue for most nonprofits is how to manage a growing organization effectively. Many founders aren't managers and don't possess a background in management. They may be "program" people who have created the nonprofit to fulfill specific goals, but management is often not one of their strengths. Sometimes the founders don't see the need for a formal organizational structure, which may hurt operations.

It's important for founders and boards of directors to realize the importance of a suitable structure and to find proper personnel or volunteers to fill out the needed spots. I've seen small organizations failing to follow their mission statements because they didn't possess a basic infrastructure, management, and personnel to deal with the necessary operating requirements.

Programs

Without programs, nonprofits can't exist. So, obviously, programs are the most important areas. As such, they must link to the organization's mission statement to be well focused and effective.

✓ **The mission statement is so important that tax Form 990 specifically requests it.**

Significance

Programs are the heart of any nonprofit. If the purpose is to help the homeless, the organization will offer programs in accordance with this goal. Such programs are likely to involve food distribution and mental health evaluation.

As nonprofits get their funding based on programs, these must be well designed and managed to earn the attention of donors and grantors, including government entities.

It can be tricky to identify programs correctly. Sometimes, a program in one place can be fundraising in another. For instance, an organization sells used clothes at a thrift shop. The thrift shop is most likely part of the fundraising area and not a program. However, if the organization provides job training for teens, then the thrift shop could be part of a program, especially if it has teens training in the shop's operations.

Managing Programs

Program management involves many issues, such as connection to the mission statement and cost issues.

Mission Statement --The clearer and simpler the mission statement, the easier it's to create major effective programs. Suppose a nonprofit's mission statement is to "provide temporary shelter to the homeless." It's simple and focused. If the organization hosts a car race as part of a program, for example, it will have troubles justifying how such a program would be linked to the mission statement.

An organization with the mission statement "helping people to become self-sufficient" is too general, increasing the chances of confusion. The more targeted the mission statement, the easier it's to develop well-directed programs.

"Mission creep" is a problem that happens when certain stakeholders want to set up programs not related to its mission statement. Donors and grantors may also cause this problem by offering funds for programs outside the scope of the organization's mission.

Program Expense Allocation- A common concern within the program section is expenses, especially when dealing with grants. **Programs don't run free, unfortunately. So, It's common for** nonprofits to classify expenses or costs into two types:

- Direct
- Indirect

Direct costs- Direct costs or expenses are easily assigned to a program, such as art supplies for an art program. The nonprofit knows for sure how much it spends on supplies for this program. There's no doubt. Direct costs are usually supported by bills and time sheets showing clearly that the expenses belong to a particular program.

Indirect costs- Indirect costs or expenses, also known as overhead, are those affecting more than one program. Organizations can't clearly identify these costs as belonging to one program or another. For example, costs of fire insurance on a building that houses all programs and operations may be considered an indirect cost.

Costs within the area of General and Administration are usually indirect, and it's common for nonprofits to allocate these costs to programs using a reasonable methodology. Often expenses are booked first in the F&A area and then are assigned to programs.

Note that the federal government has its own definition of Indirect costs and calculations, which may be different from other grantors and the nonprofit internal reporting. So, it's best to have written policies regarding program costs to avoid confusion. Many organizations use spreadsheets to keep allocations straight.

Other Considerations- The accounting system should identify direct and indirect costs, keeping program expenses separate from other sections. Nonprofits must also segregate revenues and expenses by individual programs. For example, organizations should separate supply expenses from Program A from supply expenses from Program B. This is one of the reasons the chart of accounts often has long segments--to accommodate the need to separate transactions details at many levels.

Not surprisingly, the program section is expected to report the most expenses in financial statements. Since programs are the reason for the organization's existence, donors and grantors carefully review this area as compared with the others. Are programs 80 percent of total costs? 50 percent? The higher the percentage, the better off the organization is in the eyes of donors.

Programs Challenge

Measuring Success Donors (and grantors) want to know if programs are working and if they should continue with the awards. However, measuring a program's success is a challenge for many organizations. For example, gauging the impact of a social program in a community can be tricky.

Attendance can be a sign of success in some programs, but this may not always be the case. A nonprofit may implement a hotline program, where the number of calls received is a good measuring stick. However, if the hotline's goal is to provide babysitting referrals, the number of kids placed, rather than the number of calls, would be more indicative of success.

As programs are set up, nonprofits must be aware of the question, "How can we prove the program works?" The organization may create a baseline to compare "before" and "after." Also, programs should focus on measurable goals, such as to serve 200 families or to provide food for 100 homeless people. If a program has the goal of improving the mental health of 100 men, then there must be a way to gauge not only the number of men but also the improvements within these men. These measurements can be observations and notes by clinicians or results of tests given to program participants.

To determine success properly, staff is trained in understanding the concepts and methods of gathering the required information. Otherwise, the documentation may be sloppy, and the program could lose a lot of money.

Management and General

Per Peter Drucker, *"Management is doing things right; leadership is doing the right things."* Management is the backbone of any nonprofit. It provides a structure for the programs and fundraising sections to work efficiently.

Significance

The "management and general" area is composed of all tasks not directly related to programs or fundraising. Many nonprofits call this area "Administration," "General and Administration," or "G&A." Typically, the management and general section comprises of the following:

- Planning and strategy—both long and short-term
- Accounting/finance activities, including budget preparation and financial reporting
- Human resources processes—hiring and keeping the right people, employee benefits
- Risk management—insurance issues, safety
- Legal issues—dealing with lawsuits and other legal matters
- Construction oversight and management
- Building maintenance and repairs
- IT—computer and software purchases and maintenance
- Security of assets
- Investment decisions

✓ **The G&A area typically reports the second highest expense on financial statements, after programs.**

Managing G&A

Decisions by G&A affect all functions of a nonprofit, so they must be made carefully and promptly. Major decisions involving significant expenses, including construction costs, are usually made by the board of directors, providing an extra layer of protection in this area.

An unusual duty of management is to assess individual in-kind donations—gifts of things—before they're accepted. While development staff may be involved, major in-kind donations often require the approval of G&A. A gift of land or a building seems great at first; however, upon further scrutiny, it may hold the organization responsible for cleaning up hazardous materials, or other significant costs. Typically, G&A managers accept only large donations that make sense to the organization. For instance, a nonprofit may not take a work of art because it may not be able to afford the extra insurance.

G&A may be a combination of direct and indirect costs, although it's typically considered an "indirect cost" or "overhead."

One of the issues I noticed about G&A is related to committee-based decisions. Instead of one person deciding, the organization forms a committee to perform this task. This method may not be the best for the nonprofit. For example, an organization tried to implement a new nationwide system for donations. Nobody at the executive level had the experience or the knowledge to make decisions about it. A committee, comprised of employees at different levels, formed to make significant decisions regarding the new system.

Up to a certain point, committee decisions were valid and made sense. However, the organization really needed a chief information officer to oversee this process and to make sound judgments in this situation. This person was hired after the committee made numerous bad and costly mistakes. The group-decision model may not be very effective, but it's often part of the nonprofit culture.

Administrative Challenges

Funding- A challenge to G&A is securing funding to cover its costs. Donors, especially foundations and wealthy individuals, may not want to donate for G&A, preferring all their money to go to a particular project or research. Their reluctance in allocating funds for G&A is likely due to the fear of mismanagement and fraud, and the many scandalous stories in the media regarding these cases.

Psychologically, it's more heartwarming to donate to a particular program, rather than to general operations of an organization. The result is that institutions end up having to spend other funds to cover G&A expenses. Many times galas and other fundraising efforts are used to cover those.

This problem has reached a crisis point in many places, where most funds have been restricted for programs only with nothing left over for management. As we know, without management, the nonprofit can't adequately fulfill its mission and programs; therefore, the organization may have to close if it only has program-restricted funds. To resolve this issue, donors may be required to allocate a portion of grants to G&A and overhead, or funds may not be accepted.

Due to funding cuts, some' G&A managers may decide to "borrow" funds from restricted programs to cover other areas, including administration. Nonprofits should avoid this situation because not only does it show lousy cash management, but it may also be prohibited by grant stipulations and state laws.

Allocations- Organizations allocate G&A at period-end to programs based on a logical and reasonable manner. For example, salaries may be assigned based on timesheets used for a month with information on areas people worked. Other expenses may be allocated based on square footage or another basis. According to FASB update 2016-*14 Presentation of Financial Statements of Not-for-profit Entities*, nonprofits will need to disclose the method employed on the allocations.

Another challenge is that allocations may become cumbersome with each grantor's definitions and rules, including the idea of cost pools to allocate certain costs appropriately. Many organizations prepare spreadsheets to keep the information straight, besides using the regular accounting system.

Fundraising

Nonprofits often call the fundraising function as "Development." The closest counterpart in the for-profit world would be "Marketing." However, while for-profit marketing's goal is to increase sales, developments goal is to maintain and increase donations, grants, and other income.

Significance

A nonprofit is usually not in the business of fundraising only, but it needs this functional area to maintain and increase its cash flows. The fundraising department markets the organization, searches for supporting sources, and monitors amounts received. Its staff plan and work on fundraising activities, such as golf tournaments, dinner parties, and telethons. They may write grant proposals to foundations, businesses, and governments. It's common for development people to set up seminars regarding the virtues of adding donations to estate planning.

Fundraisers are usually busy keeping current support and finding sources of aid, including business grants. This work is valuable, even if nonprofits are mostly subsidized with government grants. Often, the money from the government isn't enough to cover all overhead and other "extra" costs, so special events and other campaigns managed by fundraising are required.

Managing Fundraising

The fundraising department's goal is to make the organization's programs attractive to donors, who may be individuals, foundations, businesses, governments, or other nonprofits. Often, fundraising is about selling a new program, or improvements or changes to existing programs.

The idea is for donors to be matched with the organization's needs and programs. For instance, who would be interested in donating to a certain cause? Maybe the institution needs to obtain more funds to help the increasing homeless population—who would be interested in this program?

Fundraisers also should know about state laws since such laws regulate fundraising activities, including obtaining proper permits and issues with sales taxes.

Communications from this department should be honest and accurate, including brochures and marketing materials for campaigns and special events. Revenues from fundraising events for one cause or program should be earmarked for this restricted use and not be spent on something else.

People working in this department can make presentations, create radio and TV spots, and other promotional activities. Larger nonprofits may retain a director or vice-president of development and build an entire department dedicated to raising funds. In other organizations, this function is outsourced on an "as needed" basis. Also, many times, board members are the best fundraisers for the organization.

✓ **Nonprofits must be flexible and have the ability to accept credit card and online donations as part of fundraising efforts.**

Fundraising departments may also work with donors' employers that match donations of employees, increasing the overall funding for the organization. If an employee gives $10, the employer may match with $5, $10, or even $20.

Fundraising efforts should permeate the entire organization and not be restricted to just one department. Donors should feel welcome by everyone, not only by development personnel. So, fundraising staff may train others in how to handle prospective donors. Many times donors call the accounting department or other departments to make donations over the phone, and they should feel comfortable doing so.

Fundraising Challenges

Bad Economy- As expected, when the economy is weak, it's hard to obtain donations. Fundraisers may offer benefactors the option of contributing in installments to facilitate the process. They may also set up sweepstakes to attract more gifts.

Costs of Fundraising- Fundraising managers should be creative in decreasing the costs of campaigns and events. For example, nonprofits should take advantage of the special postal rates for tax-exempt organizations and negotiate deals with venues for events. Many places offer nonprofit discounts as well. Fundraisers should know about the sale and use-tax laws in the states where they may be exempt from paying or collecting taxes on certain transactions.

Additionally, fundraisers must consider all expenditures, including overhead, when evaluating fundraising activities. When an event is held at a separate venue, rent and other expenses are considered, but when events are held in-house, building maintenance and other not-so-obvious costs are often ignored, although they are real. To this end, some nonprofits assign a fee or a percentage to in-house events, so the expenses are realistic.

Lack of transparency- One of the problems noted with fundraising is regarding organizations raising funds for one cause and then placing the funds into a net asset with no donor restriction and using them for operations, rather than for the program originally shown. This situation is neither ethical nor fair to donors, placing the organization in a potential liability situation since donors may complain that they donated under false pretenses.

So, funds specified for a cause must be separated in the accounting system and not be mixed with other money. Many nonprofits deposit restricted cash in a separate bank account to avoid confusion

Compensation- Fundraisers may get bonuses for campaigns, but paying them a percentage of the money raised isn't advised, according to the Association of Fundraising Professionals (www.afpnet.org).

We have all heard of fundraising firms that end up keeping most of the money. They may offer to fundraise "for cheap," but end up with most of the funds. Consequently, organizations should apply due diligence when dealing with fundraising firms. Nonprofits should also avoid hiring companies belonging to board members or other related parties to avoid problems with private inurement, where one or more persons take advantage of the organization for personal gain.

✓ **Many donors don't like "over-solicitations" and can become testy. Be careful.**

<u>Summary</u>

Nonprofits usually classify operations as Programs, Administration (G&A), and Fundraising. These three sections work together for the organization to follow its mission. Programs, the heart of the nonprofit, involve direct and indirect costs.

G&A is the backbone of operations, including accounting and HR functions. A challenge here is to obtain funds to cover its expenses and the complexities of cost allocations.

Fundraising is the marketing and development of an organization. This area handles special events, donors, and grant proposals. One of its challenges is to obtain funds during a bad economy.

4 - Accounting Basics

"Money is better than poverty, if only for financial reasons."

Woody Allen

Nonprofits, like any other business, need money to survive. Good deeds can carry an organization only so far, and with the money comes the accounting practices, which are a bit different from the for-profit world. Since nonprofits aren't in the business of making a profit, accounting differences between for-profits and nonprofits warrant some discussion.

A good approach is to assume that accounting for nonprofit organizations is the same as for-profits, but with an extra level of detail. It's similar to project accounting. In the nonprofit world not all revenues are equal, and they're not recognized in the same way. Since revenue may relate to a particular program or grant, organizations need to track the source and kind of income carefully. Also, an expense isn't just an expense, as it could be related to a particular program or grant and can't be mixed with other expenditures in the accounting records. Nonprofits must track revenues and expenses in such a detailed manner that it may surprise people accustomed to the for-profit model.

This chapter will cover accounting taking in consideration the Accounting Standards Update (ASU) 2016-14 *Presentation of Financial Statements of Not-for-Profit Entities* effective for fiscal years starting on December 15, 2017. This ASU included a few changes to simplify nonprofit reporting and clarify some accounting issues. You can check this update at www.fasb.org.

GAAP

GAAP stands for "Generally Accepted Accounting Principles." These are guidelines, usually promulgated by FASB as part of the Accounting Standards Codification (ASC), to guide accounting and financial reporting in the U.S. The ASC Document 958 contains guidelines for nonprofit accounting and financial statements.

Accounting for nonprofits is also known as "fund accounting." Note that the word "fund" means different things to various people, so for our purposes in this publication, funds and net assets refer to the same thing.

The primary purpose of fund accounting (nonprofit accounting) is the stewardship of economic resources, ensuring that such resources are spent in compliance with legal or other requirements. Rather than having concerns about investors' interests, fund accounting focuses on maintaining adequate money supply to provide for present and future programs and services. The concepts and accounting issues discussed in this publication are compliant with GAAP unless mentioned otherwise.

Cash or Accrual

Accounting has two basic methods to recognize transactions—Cash and Accrual. Nonprofits have the choice of using either method, although the accrual is the one accepted by GAAP. Under the cash basis, revenue and expenses are recognized when money exchanges hands.

Therefore, when a nonprofit receives a bill, it doesn't recognize it as an expense until it's paid. On the other hand, under the accrual basis, the bill may be recognized as an expense even if it's not paid. According to the accrual method, transactions are identified as they happen, rather than when money is received or paid.

Cash Basis

The main advantage of the cash basis of accounting is that it reflects the current cash situation. It's simple. Revenues shown on financial reports are funds received, while expenses presented are those paid. Many times board members and management prefer cash basis financial statement because the

y can understand them better.

Also, cash basis accounting is conservative in recognizing revenues. If large pledges aren't collectible, the cash method may provide a more realistic view of the financial situation of the organization since it only reports on money received (and paid).

However, cash basis accounting has inherent weaknesses, such as not recognizing future revenues or expenses. This issue makes planning difficult. For instance, if the organization is supposed to pay $100,000 within the next few months, it's better to show this liability now and not be surprised later on.

Another weakness of the cash basis is that the time of revenue recognition isn't the same as expense recognition. The timing is off and may create confusion; such as when a nonprofit pays an expense of

$100,000 but hasn't received the revenue yet. At first glance, this will show the organization with a loss, but in reality, the income will be shown later on this basis of accounting.

The cash method would not be appropriate if the organization tries to estimate the cost of a program based on current expenses,, but most of the bills are paid in the future. Expenses may be "forgotten" now but may show up months later. Consequently, budgeting or reporting the programs on the cash basis may contain incomplete information.

✓ **When there are no major receivables or payables, differences between the cash and accrual basis may not be material.**

Many small nonprofits employ the cash basis and then make adjustments to bring it to accrual basis at year-end, usually with outside auditors' assistance.

Accrual Basis

We have many good reasons for a nonprofit to report on an accrual basis, rather than on a cash basis. Not only is the accrual method accepted by GAAP, but it's also endorsed by the IFRS—International Financial Reporting Standards. These international standards guide many companies worldwide, including the U.S., which is in the process of adopting them. The IFRS may not have much effect now on U.S. nonprofits, but it's just a matter of time before its requirements will start trickling down to the nonprofit sector.

An advantage of the accrual method is the matching of revenues to expenses, giving users a better view of the economic condition of an organization. When an event occurs, for instance, revenues and expenses for the event are shown together by using accounts payable, receivable, deferred revenues and other items not employed on the cash basis of accounting.

Another benefit of accrual accounting is that it includes many useful reports. For example, if an organization shows $300,000 in revenue and is on the accrual basis, the aging of receivables report would be helpful to determine the details of amounts still owed to the nonprofit.

However, the accrual basis, with its technical concepts such as deferred revenue, can be complicated for non-accountants to understand. Usually, when presenting an accrual report to managers who aren't knowledgeable about accounting, I explain how much of the revenues showing up are still owed and how much of the expenses have been paid. An example of a report using cash and accrual methods is shown next.

The Do-Good Organization
Statement of Financial Position
December 31, 20X1

		Cash Basis	Accrual Basis
Assets			
	Cash	10,000	10,000
	Interest receivable	0	3,000
	Pledges receivable	0	5,000
Total Assets:		10,000	18,000
Liabilities			
	Accrued expenses	0	7,000
Net Assets Without Donor Restrictions		10,000	11,000
Total Liabilities and Net Assets:		10,000	18,000

This report shows accrued (unpaid) expense of $7,000 that is significant to the organization. It also indicates that the accrual basis of accounting would benefit the nonprofit in managing its finances. If managers only review the cash numbers, they will be misled and will not be aware of the accrued expenses – those that will be paid in the future. An accrual could be an estimate for utilities bill -- services provided in one period and paid in the future.

Nonprofits may also employ a modified accrual basis where revenues are recognized when received, and expenses are on the accrual basis, showing as payables. This setup seems to be a conservative approach, but it's not compliant with GAAP and is usually brought up to full accrual at year-end with auditors' help.

Net Assets

Nonprofits' financial statements utilize a different vocabulary than for-profits' with terms like "Net Assets" that may puzzle some readers. Net asset, also known as a fund, is a basic concept for an organization. While for-profit financial statements present retained earnings, nonprofits show net assets.

A net asset is like a "bucket." Nonprofits place each revenue and expense in a particular bucket. For instance, if an organization has $100 in postage expenses, the question is not only about which account to use, but also which net asset (bucket) the expense belongs to. If there are departments, then the amount needs to be booked in the right account, department, and net asset. This is a lot of information to be captured, often requiring nonprofits to have accounts with many digits to keep it all straight.

Some organizations create various restricted net assets, one for each purpose, to keep things straight. For example, money received for buying books are recognized in a separate net asset from money received to support a travel program. Each of these programs has its own net asset. Other nonprofits keep historical spreadsheets on what each net asset or fund contains. Many do both because it's too easy to "forget" money received. Be aware of this common problem—a typical issue for many nonprofits.

Due to the detail level in fund accounting, a "roll-forward schedule, a common annual report, is required. The report shows the beginning balances of all net assets and transactions, as well as the ending balances. An example of this type of schedule is next:

Roll Forward - Restricted Net Assets Worksheet				Year 20XX	
Segment #		Beg. Balance	Increases	Decreases	End. Balance
503	Scholarship	100,000	40,000	(15,000)	125,000
504	Books	50,000	3,000	(1,000)	52,000
509	Building	125,000	--	(30,000)	95,000
	Total Restricted	275,000	43,000	(46,000)	272,000

Some nonprofits keep separate checking accounts for each net asset and reconcile the balances with the accounting books at least once a year. The point is to remember all monies and to spend them appropriately.

Net Asset Types

Net assets provide a structure for the organization to identify and track different types of revenues and expenses. They organize the accounting data so that queries and reporting can be done easily.

SFAS 117, used to be the official guidance on this topic. Now, FASB Accounting Standards Codification (ASC) provides the rules for this sector. Consequently, you may see references to both SFAS and ASC when researching nonprofit financial issues. The idea is to identify, classify and report on funds and not "bunch" them all together. Note that this area has been changed a bit with the FASB update 2016-14 *Presentation of Financial Statements of Not-for-Profit Entities*, effective December 2017, covered here.

✓ **Net assets or funds aren't "assets."**

Nonprofit management may consider net assets as projects with their own financial statements. Net assets, also known as assets less liabilities, are mechanisms to keep the financial information straight over the long term. To this end, an organization may have more than one type of net asset to handle its operations. The basic types of net assets are:

- Net Assets Without Donor Restrictions

- Net Assets With Donor Restrictions

Before the FASB update 2016-14, three net assets were presented in the financial statements:

o   Unrestricted Net Asset

o   Temporarily Restricted Net Asset

o   Permanently Restricted Net Asset

Combined as Net Assets With Donor Restrictions

Overall, the three types of net assets can still be employed internally to keep transactions straight. Although temporarily restricted and permanently restricted net assets are combined under one heading, their goals and usage are different; it doesn't make sense to combine them in the accounting setup.

So, consider the net assets with donor restrictions as an "umbrella" for temporarily and permanently restricted funds, used in the official financial statements to make them easier to understand. Temporarily and permanently restricted net assets still exist as separate elements and should be maintained as before. Just the reporting changed.

✓   **All transactions are recognized in one of these net assets with no exceptions.**

See next an excerpt of the Statement of Activities, a report showing revenues and expenses:

The Helping Organization
Statement of Activities
Year ended December 31, 20xx

		Net Assets Without Donor Restrictions	Net Assets With Donor Restrictions	Total
Revenue				
	Contributions	100,000	70,000	170,000
	Fees for service	55,000		55,000
	~	~	~	~
	~	~	~	~
	~	~	~	~
Ending Net Asset Balance		250,000	50,000	320,000

The Net Assets with Donor Restrictions is made up of

Temporarily Restricted Net Assets Contributions-- $50,000

Permanently Restricted Net Assets Contributions - $20,000

The example shows the Helping Organization receiving $100,000 in contributions, booked in the Net Assets without Donor Restrictions to be spent in daily activities. Of the Net Assets Restricted by Donor, the contribution of $50,000 is temporarily restricted to be used in the future or for a specific program. The $20,000 most likely, is an endowment to be held long term, while the nonprofit can spend income, such as interest.

Net Assets without Donor Restrictions

This net asset, also known as "unrestricted" following "old" guidance, is employed to run operations, day-to-day activities, and general transactions of the organization. Nonprofits may also call this net asset as "Unrestricted," "Current Unrestricted Fund," or "Operating Net Asset." If an organization has donations with no restrictions, these will show here. As an example, suppose a nonprofit receives $10,000 to fund current activities. The amount is booked as revenue in this unrestricted net asset.

Donations for a particular activity, not part of general operations, such as a new food program for the homeless, aren't booked into this net asset. Rather, they are included in the net asset restricted by donor.

✓ **Most expenses run through the net asset without donor restriction, even though revenues may be booked in another net asset, such as temporarily restricted.**

An interesting subset of the net asset without donor restrictions is the "Board Designated Fund." Boards can designate funds to pay for individual projects. An example would be a "generosity fund" set up by the board for specific programs. The board could also change its mind and decide to spend the funds on something else. This fund is part of the unrestricted net asset "umbrella" and not restricted, as only donors can restrict funds, not boards.

According to ASU 2016-14, effective for fiscal years starting after December 15, 2017, board designated funds are presented as part of the financial statements disclosures in an effort for users to assess the liquidity, the cash flows, of an organization. Unfortunately, nonprofits may have millions in restricted revenues, but not enough funds to meet payroll. So, now organizations must disclose all limitations on cash and prove that it can fulfill its financial obligations a year from the financial statements date. So, any amounts earmarked for specific projects or designated by the board must be disclosed, even if they are unrestricted.

Note that the net assets without donor restrictions are significant not just for operations, but for debt covenants as well. Many banks require a minimum balance in the unrestricted assets as part of loans or bonds deals.

Net Assets With Donor Restrictions

This net asset classification is made up of two "old" net assets that are combined in the official financial statements. Since the two have different goals, we are covering them separately here—temporarily and permanently restricted net assets.

1- Temporarily Restricted Net Assets

Nonprofits call this net asset a "Restricted Net Asset," "Restricted Fund," or "Temporarily Restricted Fund." They use this net asset for a particular purpose, as per the donors' wishes, which can't be changed by the board of directors. If a donor wants the money to go for brain cancer research only, board members can't override this wish and apply the funds toward publications, for instance. As expected, donors should approve any changes.

✓ **When you read or hear about restricted net assets or funds, it usually refers to the temporarily restricted net asset.**

Organizations should exercise due diligence, including maintaining written documentation to justify the restrictions and comply with donors' wishes. If a donor doesn't want to put anything in writing, the organization could send a "thank you" note confirming the situation.

Such supporters can restrict funds for a specific activity, program, event, etc. However, there are limits. Many nonprofits implement policies about this issue to avoid confusion. Suppose a donor gives $100 to a program that doesn't exist. Should the organization return the funds to the donor? Should it recognize the donation in another similar program? Policies and procedures should cover these topics in detail to guide both the donors and the nonprofit on how to handle these situations. Supporters should be aware of such documentation as well for proper transparency.

Many organizations maintain more than one temporarily restricted asset to help in managing such "buckets." They may have one net asset for donations related to scholarship and another one for a reading program. Both may be reported together, but are kept separate in the accounting system.

A significant restricted activity may involve several stages, as it's the case with a capital campaign for construction. Some donors want to donate after construction has started, while others would like to give to a particular room or classroom. In this case, separate subaccounts within the temporarily restricted capital campaign "umbrella" could be set up.

Many times the donation is for the future, and the restriction is about timing or reimbursement of expenses. Once the restriction is lifted, revenue is "released." As an example, suppose a donor gives $10,000 to defray expenses of a travel program for a school. The $10,000 is booked in the restricted net asset. As travel expenditures occur, revenue is released from temporarily restricted to the unrestricted net asset, "refunding" the unrestricted net asset for the costs. See next a summary of the transactions assuming the expenses occurred $5,000 at a time.

	Net Assets Without Donor Restrictions	Temp. Restricted Net Asset- part of Net Assets With Donor Restrictions
Donation to restricted net asset		10,000 increase revenue
Travel Expenses 1	5,000 increase expense	
Release from restriction	5,000 increase revenue	5,000 decrease revenue
Travel Expenses 2	5,000 increase expense	
Release from restriction	5,000 increase revenue	5,000 decrease revenue
Net Asset Balance	No effect	0 balance

Once the organization incurs $10,000 in travel expenses, the balance in the restricted net asset would be zero. The total effect on the unrestricted asset will be zero because restricted money covered the expenses

An example of a timing restriction is a donation that can be spent only in the future because of a special anniversary. In this case, expenses don't matter. For example, a donor gives $5,000 to commemorate a tenth anniversary. On the day of the anniversary, the amount is released regardless of expenses incurred. A release based on timing is "extra" unrestricted money the organization can spend as it sees fit. In contrast, a release to reimburse expenses isn't extra since it was already spent.

✓ **Don't forget to look at the restricted net assets for budgeting— revenues classified there may cover significant costs.**

Organizations release net assets up to the balance in the restricted net assets. If a restricted net asset has a net asset balance of $20,000, then the organization can release up to $20,000 only. If a nonprofit doesn't have any restricted net assets, there is no need to release anything.

✓ **Balances on restricted net assets can't be negative.**

Overall, restricted net asset balances should decrease as revenues are used up, and net assets should be released as time progresses or expenses occur, depending on the restriction. The idea is for all temporarily restricted net assets to zero out over time. If a net asset balance is negative, it's a sign of error since nonprofits can't release/decrease revenues they don't have.

2- Permanently Restricted Net Assets

Many people leave money to a charity in their names or in their family's names as long-term gifts or endowments, often as part of estate planning. The idea is for the donation's principal to remain intact, while the organization is allowed to spend any income, such as dividends. Nonprofits recognize this gift type in the permanently restricted net asset, also known as an "endowment fund."

Permanently restricted net asset is combined with the temporarily restricted net asset and shown as one under the "Net assets With Donor Restriction" designation.

This net asset is often large and held in perpetuity, or for a very long time. Traditionally, the larger the endowment fund, the stronger the organization's economic situation. Colleges are known for their large endowments with Harvard University endowment, one of the front-runners, having about $35.7 billion in 2016.

Many states have adopted the UPMIFA (Uniform Prudent Management of Institutional Funds Act), which provides uniform rules related to endowment investments and expenses. Nonprofits should check with the states where they operate for specific laws regarding this type of donation as some states allow for an inflation/deflation effect on investments, while others don't.

As far as accounting is concerned, we have the ASU 2016-*14 Presentation of Financial Statements of Not-for-profit Entities,* a FASB update that covers the treatment of "underwater" endowments, i.e. funds that lost value as compared to original donation date. Any losses are reported under the Net Assets With Donor Restrictions. Before this ASU became effective, the nonprofit recognized this loss as part of unrestricted net assets. Additional disclosures are also required with endowments as per this ASU.

It's important to keep all documentation on permanently restricted net assets safe, as sometimes the income from such funds is for specific programs or could be used for administration. Since nonprofits keep the money in this net asset for a very long time, the documentation must be protected and available for the long-term.

An unfortunate situation has happened to some nonprofits, where they had money in endowments, but not in unrestricted net assets, and had to borrow from the permanently restricted net asset to cover for day-to-day activities. Not a good sign. A few organizations had to close or merge after such loans.

See a summary of net assets next:

Net Assets Without Donor Restrictions	Shows most expenses	Balance increases with "releases"
Temporarily Restricted- Net Assets with Donor Restrictions	Shows no expenses with a few exceptions	Balance decreases with "releases"
Permanently Restricted – Net Assets with Donor Restrictions	Principal can't be spent	UPMIFA applies along with ASU 2016-14

Inter-fund Accounts

Inter-fund accounts link all net assets. These accounts carry standard names to identify them quickly, such as "Due to" and "Due from." They're similar to the interdepartmental or inter-company accounts in the for-profit world. The inter-fund accounts are employed to keep track of loans and any transactions between the net assets. Like their for-profit counterparts, they're internal entries that total up to zero at the consolidated level.

Suppose a nonprofit has more than one net asset without donor restrictions, such as an unrestricted and an unrestricted- board-designated net asset. If the unrestricted net asset borrows money from the designated one, "Due to/Due from" accounts are utilized to document the transaction. These accounts help to keep all net assets straight with many nonprofits zeroing them out before year-end to avoid confusion.

Net Assets Released from Restrictions Accounts

These inter-fund accounts are typical of the nonprofit sector with some similarity to the deferred revenue account (liability) used in the for-profit business. However, in the nonprofit world, a donation received that can't be spent right away (restricted) is recognized as part of the restricted net asset, not as deferred revenue.

When the restriction is met, the "Net Assets Released from Restrictions" accounts, also known as "release accounts," are employed to decrease the restricted net asset and increase the unrestricted net asset. This process is a bit similar to reducing the deferred revenue and increasing the income in the for-profit world.

The "release" is presented in the Statement of Activities (Income Statement of nonprofits) as a positive number under the unrestricted net asset column and as a negative number under the temporarily restricted net asset column. Both positive and negative numbers should be the same and zero out when added up together.

Nonprofits should do these releasing entries often to keep the net asset balance numbers correct. Otherwise, the unrestricted net asset is likely to be understated, and the temporarily restricted one could be overstated.

The journal entry to release funds is to debit the temporarily restricted net asset and credit the unrestricted one. Below is an example of a release entry of $300.

Release of net assets- Restricted	300	
Release of net assets- Unrestricted		300

After the entry is booked, the temporarily restricted net assets decrease, while the unrestricted net assets increase by $300.

✓ **Release accounts are used for donations only, not for exchanges.**

Some organizations present detailed release information on financial statements, such as "Expiration of time restriction- United Way," so the release section may have more than one line, but it should always zero out across.

See next an example of a Statement of Activities, the summarized nonprofit "Income Statement" showing the release as part of revenue. Note the line on Net assets released—the total across is zero.

Do-good Organization
Statement of Activities
As of December 31, 20XX

	Net Assets Without Restriction	Net Assets With Donor Restrictions	Total
REVENUES			
Contributions	3,050	6,000	9,050
Fundraising activities	500	300	800
Professional programs	100		100
Net assets released	300	(300)	
TOTAL REVENUES	3,950	6,000	9,950
EXPENSES			
Programs:			
Program A	350		350
Program B	220		220
Program C	150		150
Management and General	500		500
Fundraising	100		100
TOTAL EXPENSES	1,320		1,320
Change in net assets	2,630	6,000	8,630
Net Assets at beg. of year	2,500	500	3,000
Net Assets at end of year	5,130	6,500	11,630

Nonprofits employ release accounts because

o   Specific expenses occurred, or

o   A particular date arrived.

Examples of entries illustrating both situations are next.

Example of release entry to cover expenses- Organization bought $500 worth of literacy books. Donations for such books were recognized in a restricted net asset. Cash for this expenditure came out of the unrestricted net asset checking account, where all cash is deposited.

Relevant journal entries would be:

JE-1	GF- Book Expense	500	
	GF- Cash		500
	To buy books covered by restricted net asset		

JE-2	RF- Net assets released from restrictions	500	
	GF- Net assets released from restrictions		500
	To release revenue restricted		

GF- General-Unrestricted net assets
RF- Temporarily Restricted net assets

See an excerpt of a Statement of Activities after these transactions occurred:

		Net Assets Without Donor Restrictions	Net Assets With Donor Restrictions
Revenues			
	Contributions		
	Other Income		
	Net Assets released from restriction	500	(500.00)
Total Revenues		500	(500.00)
Expenses			
	Program- Literacy Books	500	
	Management and General		
	Fund Raising		
Total Expenses		500	
Change in net assets		0	(500.00)

Note that the end result with the unrestricted net asset (net assets without restrictions) is zero while the transactions decreased the restricted net asset by $500. As expected, this statement shows no expenses for the restricted net asset, only for unrestricted.

Example of release entries for timing- The organization received $10,000 for use only after Mary's birthday, which is today. The nonprofit has had this amount on the books since 2001, but it could not spend it until today. The journal entry today will be:

RF-Net assets released from restriction   10,000

          GF-Net assets released from restriction   10,000

To release funds initially restricted by date.

GF- General Net Asset
RF- Restricted Net Asset

When net assets are released due to timing, the money may be available for any expense. Nonprofits can spend it for any purpose. The result is that the unrestricted net asset increases because no expenses are associated with this donation. See next an excerpt of a Statement of Activities after this journal entry:

	Net Assets Without Donor Restrictions	Net Assets With Donor Restrictions
Revenues		
Contributions		
Other Income		
Net Assets released from restriction	10,000	(10,000)
Total Revenues	10,000	(10,000)
Expenses		
Program- Literacy		
Books		
Management and General		
Fund Raising		
Total Expenses		-
Change in net assets	10,000	(10,000)

Documentation on the restrictions is essential. Some organizations keep releases from restrictions on a separate spreadsheet with details, while others add to the description of the account or transaction. If documentation gets lost, contact the donor for duplicates or updates.

Since this official presentation can be confusing, many board members prefer to see details of the expenses as part of each net asset instead of a one-line item. Therefore, many organizations recognize the expenses on each temporarily restricted net asset, and at year-end, they adjust the numbers to comply with GAAP. See next examples of an organization's financial statements before and after adjustments.

Before—internal use only—using pre-ASU 2016-14 presentation- Not GAAP

Internal Report of ABC Nonprofit
December 31, 20XX

	Unrestricted	Temporarily Restricted	Permanently Restricted	Total
Changes to Unrestricted Net Assets:				
Revenues and Gains:				
Public Contributions (net)	430,000		50,000	480,000
Investment Income	14,780			14,780
Net Assets Released from Restrictions	-		-	-
Total Revenues, Gains and other Support:	444,780	-	50,000	494,780
Total Expenses and Losses:				
Programs				-
Books		5,490		5,490
Scholarships		10,000		10,000
General Administration	125,000	-		125,000
Fundraising	20,000	-		20,000
Total Expenses and Losses:	145,000	15,490		160,490
Increase/Decrease in Net Assets	299,780	(15,490)	50,000	334,290
Net Assets at Beginning of Year	100,000	150,000	500,000	750,000
Net Assets at End of Year	399,780	134,510	550,000	1,084,290

This report shows expenses of $15,490 charged to each net asset for books and scholarships. Note that there was $150,000 as the beginning balance in the temporarily restricted net assets, so recognizing the expense amounts in this net asset type seems to be appropriate, although not presented according to GAAP.

You can see next the same report using GAAP rules. The idea is still the same, but the nonprofit shows the release within the revenue area.

Note that when FASB ASU 2016-14 becomes effective, we only have two net assets columns: Net Assets Without Donor Restrictions (Unrestricted) and Net Assets With Donor Restrictions (temporarily + permanently net assets combined)

After—Official format using ASU 2016-14 presentation and GAAP

ABC Nonprofit
Statement of Activities
December 31, 20XX

	Net Assets Without Donor Restrictions	Net Assets With Donor Restrictions	Total
Changes to Unrestricted Net Assets:			
Revenues and Gains:			
Public Contributions (net)	430,000	50,000	480,000
Investment Income	14,780		14,780
Net Assets Released from Restrictions	15,490	(15,490)	-
Total Revenues, Gains and other Support:	460,270	34,510	494,780
Total Expenses and Losses:			
Programs			
Books	5,490		5,490
Scholarships	10,000		10,000
General Administration	125,000	-	125,000
Fundraising	20,000	-	20,000
Total Expenses and Losses:	160,490	-	160,490
Increase/Decrease in Net Assets	299,780	34,510	334,290
Net Assets at Beginning of Year	100,000	650,000	750,000
Net Assets at End of Year	399,780	684,510	1,084,290

Overall, the ending balances in each net asset didn't change. For instance, the restricted net assets column shows the balance of $684,510 ($134,510+$550,000) regardless of which method is employed. Besides combining all restricted net assets in one column, the other differences between the two reports, are the expenses presentation and the "Net Assets Released from Restrictions."

When comparing the two examples, you may notice that the $15,490 in net asset release is the sum of the books and scholarships expenses on the non-GAAP report. This means that the unrestricted net asset spent the money and was "credited" by the restricted net asset.

Some institutions implement a policy of recognizing restricted revenue as unrestricted when the expenses are expected to happen during the same year to facilitate accounting. Instead of the nonprofit identifying temporarily restricted revenue and then releasing it throughout the year, accounting just considers the money as unrestricted and documents it to be able to show its release in the "official" financial statements.

Even though FASB requires only two net asset classifications, nonprofits should continue to separate the net assets three ways to avoid confusion and combine the restricted funds only for official financial presentation.

Chart of Accounts

The chart of accounts should be able to accommodate many net assets, inter-fund receivables/payables, financial, grant, and 990 reporting. Actually, many organizations create their chart of accounts following the line items in the 990, which is usually good enough. However, nonprofits may have additional needs, requiring more details and a different chart setup.

When setting up accounts, segments must be considered carefully. For instance, a "1" at the beginning of an account may point to the account belonging to an unrestricted – without donor restrictions net asset. A "2" would mean the account is temporarily restricted. Then, the next two digits could be used to identify each temporarily restricted net asset—01 would be Scholarship, 02 would be Construction, 03 would be Books. A restricted account for construction donations would look like this: 2-02-xxxx-xxx.

Some charts of accounts aren't set up correctly, with disastrous results. Unrestricted and restricted net assets should be identified in the chart of accounts level, not just in reporting. I've seen a nonprofit with a chart of accounts with no easily identifiable temporarily restricted net assets. Instead, the staff had to select accounts manually for reporting. Problems started when certain accounts were "forgotten," and net asset balances were incorrect.

Note that if a nonprofit uses a "project" or "grant" accounting module, or "class" setup, the chart of accounts can be more general since a lot of information is picked up by the module or class.

Also, the chart of accounts should be established to compile data for all reports required, such as for donors or sales taxes. There's a fine line between having an efficient chart of accounts and one that's cumbersome to maintain. Nonprofits should take the time to evaluate their needs and design a chart of accounts that works long term.

At year-end, income and expenses are closed into their own net assets, which are similar to retained earnings in the sense that they accumulate information. So, unrestricted revenue would close into net assets without donor restrictions account; restricted and permanently restricted accounts close into their own net assets accounts too.

<u>Summary</u>

Financial statements can be prepared using the cash or accrual method of accounting, with the accrual style being more accepted because it includes accounts receivable and payable. The accrual method is recognized by GAAP and should be used in official financial statements.

Instead of retained earnings, nonprofit shows net assets that accumulate and organize financial information. Most expenses are shown in the net assets without donor restrictions, while restricted revenues are presented in the net assets with donor restrictions. The net assets released from restrictions accounts are used once the restrictions are lifted.

5 - Revenue Types and Issues

"May your charity increase as much as your wealth."

Proverb

All businesses must obtain revenues to survive and pay their bills. Unlike for-profit companies where income comes from sales or billings, nonprofit organizations' revenues come from other sources such as grants and donations. These different types of income need to be reported separately, creating a very detailed and complex accounting situation.

According to the National Center for Charitable Statistics, "in 2013, public charities reported over $1.74 trillion in total revenues and $1.63 trillion in total expenses. Of the revenue:

- o 21% came from contributions, gifts and government grants.

- o 72% came from program service revenues, which include government fees and contracts.

- o 7% came from "other" sources including dues, rental income, special event income, and gains or losses from goods sold."

Depending on the nature of the revenue, nonprofits may classify it as "contribution" or "exchange."

Contribution or Exchange

A contribution or donation is a voluntary unconditional transfer of assets where the donor receives no correlated benefit. It's a straight gift. Donors may impose restrictions on the contribution, but they're not beneficiaries of the restrictions, not receiving anything of value in return. As far as accounting is concerned, nonprofits recognize contributions as revenues when received or pledged.

The other type of revenue, exchange, is a gift where the donor receives something valuable in return, such as a fee for seminars or tuition for school. In this situation, the people receive something in return, similar to a for-profit business sale. Exchanges may or may not be recognized as revenues when received or pledged, depending on the situation. Issues pointing to an exchange are:

- Financial penalties if the terms of the agreement aren't met
- Donor specifies the place and time of the program
- There is a possibility of a "profit margin"
- Donor receives direct benefits from the organization

- The nonprofit offers a specific program, rather than doing activities that would benefit the public in general

According to FASB ASU 2014- 09 *Revenue from Contracts with Customers*, the term "exchange" is called a "contract with a customer," but the concept is still about the same. This ASU is effective for nonprofits with fiscal years starting on December 15, 2018, although some with bonds outstanding need to implement it for years starting on December 15, 2017. You can read this update at the FASB website at:

http://www.fasb.org/jsp/FASB/Page/SectionPage&cid=1176156316498

Besides the change in terminology, the ASU 2014-09 requires contracts to be analyzed and the amounts recognized as revenue once the contract is fulfilled, depending on facts and circumstances.

Next is an example showing both the "old" and the ASU 2014-19 method.

An organization received a straight donation from a business for $10,000 for any purpose. It also received another check for $10,000 to pay for seminar fees. The seminar was worth $10,000. The nonprofit will classify these two checks differently:

- The first check has no strings attached and is considered to be a contribution or a donation.

- The second check has strings attached; the donor will receive something in return. The payment is an exchange, not a donation.

✓ **There are no releases of net assets on exchanges.**

The first check, a contribution, will be shown on the Statement of Activities (Income Statement of nonprofits) under net assets without donor restrictions (unrestricted). If the donor sets up any restrictions, then the organization would present it under the net assets with donor restrictions (temporarily restricted).

The second check, the exchange, will be shown on the Statement of Position (Balance Sheet of nonprofits) as deferred revenue or as "contract liability" under ASU 2014-09. Once the seminar happens, the organization recognizes the entire $10,000 revenue as unrestricted on the Statement of Activities.

Summary of contributions and exchange treatment

Type of revenue	When received for future use:
Donation	Increase Revenue- Net Asset with Donor Restriction (Temporarily restricted)
Exchange	Increase Deferred Revenue, like in for-profit. *Increase Contract Liability after ASU 2014-09 goes into effect*
Type of revenue	When activity happens:
Donation	Release of Net Asset with Donor Restrictions(Temporarily restricted) into Unrestricted Net Assets
Exchange	Decrease Deferred Revenue and recognize revenue — *Decrease Contract Liability after ASU 2014-09 goes into effect.*

Overall, the revenue is the same before and after ASU- 2014-09, but the timing is different. Also, under the update, the liability number may increase, impacting any covenant or bank deals. If this is going to be material, contact your bank and other parties about this situation.

✓ **Since the ASU 2014-09 requirements are retroactive, including more issues than covered here, nonprofits should check with their accountants about their own situation ASAP.**

The AICPA released a file with a detailed plan to help businesses:

http://www.aicpa.org/InterestAreas/FRC/AccountingFinancialRepor ting/RevenueRecognition/DownloadableDocuments/2014- 09_LIPlan.pdf

Donations of Cash, Checks, and Credit Cards

Many donors give gifts in the form of cash, checks, or credit cards. Organizations recognize such gifts for their own value, so when a nonprofit receives a check for $100, accounting recognizes it as an increase in cash and as a type of revenue. If the money is for general use, then the unrestricted revenue is booked; if the purpose is for a particular program, the temporarily restricted (with donor restriction) revenue is used and released later on.

These donations could also be contributions or exchanges with FASB ASU 2014-09 applicable after fiscal years starting on December 15, 2018

Since cash and checks are easy to lose, they must be deposited in the bank right away. Many banks allow for online deposit of checks, making this process easier. Pictures of checks can also be taken from inside the banks' app on iPhone or iPad, making it the perfect deposit solution when a nonprofit receives only a few checks a week. Payments in cash must be discouraged whenever possible to avoid the risk of loss and misappropriation.

Dealing with donations can be a problem in times of appeal or other fundraising events. A strategy should be in place for the donations to be put in a safe place ASAP. I've been to events where envelopes containing pledges, checks, and cash were thrown in the trash by mistake. So, have a group of people responsible for picking all types of donations and putting them in a safe place right away. A common control is to have more than one person counting the cash before it's deposited.

Also, before any campaign or marketing material goes out, someone from the accounting staff should look at it. I've seen marketing materials going out without a space for credit card expiration dates, creating confusion and loss of income. Accountants are usually detailed-oriented and would be able to catch these problems before it's too late.

Stock Donations

Nonprofits may receive stocks as donations, as many people donate shares as part of a tax savings strategy. These are especially popular in December.

To safeguard the stocks or to cash them, an organization needs to work with a brokerage firm. Such firm follows the decisions of the nonprofit investment committee (part of the board) that manages and monitors investments, usually in a conservative way.

Besides committees, many organizations have policies about stock donations—some hold on to the stocks, others sell it right away, and still, others leave the decisions to their brokers based on certain parameters or goals. The idea is to maximize the stock value.

The assessment of stock donations follows FASB 157 (ASC 820) regarding investments' valuation. This ASC includes guidance of alternative-type investments that are inherently riskier and may be part of the nonprofit's portfolio.

Overall, stock donations are booked as assets and organizations should:

1. Report at current fair value any equity investments that have readily determinable fair values; and

2. Show any gains or losses in the Statement of Activities, one of the standard financial statements.

✓ **Nonprofits give donors receipts for stock donations using the market value on the day of receipt of donation.**

Suppose shares are given to satisfy pledge commitments. The next step is to get the fair market value of the stocks to verify if proceeds would fulfill the obligation, as the actual value may be more or less than the pledges. It's common for donors to be contacted regarding any surplus or deficits related to the commitment and stock donations.

✓ **Any gains or losses, dividends, etc. are to be booked as investment transactions after the stock donation is made.**

Realized and unrealized gains and losses are booked the year they happen, and in the net asset they belong to.

If a nonprofit receives significant stock donations and can influence a firm's financial and operating policies, then the equity method of accounting is to be employed. This situation is handled the same way as if the nonprofit were a for-profit firm.

Gifts of stocks may be classified as temporarily or permanently restricted donation depending on donor's wishes. Other GAAP and UPMIFA rules also apply here based on the nature of the donation. These donations could also be contributions or exchanges with FASB ASU 2014-09 applicable after fiscal years starting on December 15, 2018. (Investment income and gains aren't parts of this ASU, but the original recognition of a stock donation as an exchange is.)

According to ASU 2016-14, any losses on "endowment-underwater funds," those that the initial value is lower than the current value, must be shown under the permanently restricted area—net assets with donor restrictions. Before this ASU, losses were classified as unrestricted.

Pledges Receivable

Most nonprofit organizations are familiar with pledges, as people, businesses, and foundations make promises to give in the future. Many times these promises are the results of fundraising campaigns or appeals. Depending on the situation, the pledge could be for a general or specific purpose, such as for a new child-care program.

Pledges, both short and long-term, may be shown as "Pledges" or "Unconditional Promises to Give" on the Statement of Position.

Promises to give may or may not be real. For example, if a person notifies an organization that he is including the nonprofit in his will, this isn't a pledge. The same situation exists if someone promises to pay a certain amount twenty years in the future—it's not a pledge. In both cases, donors can easily change their minds; circumstances can change, making the promises hard to keep.

✓ **Promises to give must have no conditions to be recognized as real pledges**.

Note that conditions are different from restrictions:

o   Conditions determine if the amount will be given or not

o   Restrictions determine how to use the proceeds

Suppose there is a condition associated with a pledge -- the money will be given only if a relative recovers from a serious disease. In this situation, the nonprofit records the pledge only after the condition is met, that is, the person recovers. This situation is tricky since a lot can change, and it makes good sense not to recognize this promise until it's paid. Same if the condition is the occurrence of a major disaster in California--- this pledge is conditional, and the nonprofit should not record it. Once a disaster hits California, then the pledge may be valid. Managers should use common sense here.

Another example of a condition is a company matching donations made by employees. If an employee gives $10, the firm would also pay $10, matching the donor's amount. As the employee donates, the condition on the firm's pledge is lifted. Therefore, each time an employee pays, the organization recognizes a matching pledge.

The wording of a pledge is crucial to determine when a promise is conditional or just restricted. The key word in conditional pledges is "if." Those are usually not recorded as real pledges by the nonprofit, although they may be filed for future follow up.

Once a pledge is determined to be valid, it can be unrestricted or restricted to a particular time or event, such as for a reading program happening in the future. The classification depends on donors' intentions. A pledge made on a general appeal can be safely assumed to be unrestricted, while others specific to an individual program should be considered restricted.

Organizations must have pledge documents in writing whenever possible. If a donor doesn't want to acknowledge the pledge, a thank you letter confirming the gift is a good idea. The letter can be simple and brief but should leave no doubt about the existence of the pledge and its intent.

Issues usually associated with pledges are collectability, pledges paid in installments and privacy of donors, all discussed next.

Collectability

As promises are to give in the future, pledges may not be all collectible, and most organizations aren't going to sue to collect promised amounts because of PR issues. Therefore, by its nature, pledges are riskier than regular accounts receivable. As expected, a pledge due in a year is less risky than another one due in two or more years since a lot can happen in a year or longer. Fundraising staff usually follow up on promises to pay, diplomatically, of course.

Due to the risk of default on pledges receivable, an Allowance for Uncollectible Pledges account is employed. It may be created and adjusted every year based on history. If an organization experiences 15 percent in uncollectible pledges, for instance, this percentage may be applied. It's the same concept as the Allowance for Uncollectible Receivables in the for-profit world.

A strange situation with promises to give has popped up recently with a young, wealthy supporter promising to give a significant amount to an organization. As expected, people got excited, made a public PR deal with the pledge and started planning how to spend the money. Low-and-behold -- it was all fake. The guy liked the attention, but was not wealthy and had no intention to fulfill the promise. The organization lost a lot of credibility with this deal. So, I recommend that nonprofits set up policies and procedures to evaluate significant pledges and to refrain from announcing it and making plans for it until all checks out.

Installments

Besides lump sum promises, nonprofits could also have pledges payable in installments; for example, a commitment of $25,000 payable at $5,000 a year for five years. In this case, organizations are to discount the payments to present value using a reasonable percentage. The discount is amortized as in the for-profit world. FASB ASC 820-10 (FASB 157) relates to this topic to be sure organizations evaluate pledges in a fair and acceptable manner.

✓ **Government and other grants aren't considered to be pledges and are presented separately in financial statements.**

So, if an organization receives a pledge for $30,000 payable in 5 years, apart is considered to be current pledge receivable, and the rest is non-current. In addition, revenue is recognized along with a discount plus the allowance account may be changed. Don't double count pledges – once as revenue when the promise is made and again when payments are made.

Privacy

Many times big donors want to keep their donations and personal information private. To this end, nonprofits should implement proper care so that the donor is acknowledged, donations are recorded, and the donor's identity is kept secret. So, to assure privacy, donor databases need to be kept secure. Only a few people should possess access to the donors' records.

As an example, a nonprofit organization I worked with had celebrities donating significant amounts of money, and they didn't want their names, email addresses or other information available. Therefore, instead of inputting the real names and information in the database, the organization used the names "Anonymous 1," "Anonymous 2," etc. The nonprofit kept the real names and personal information under lock and key in a file cabinet accessible only by a couple of people. This low-tech setup worked well.

Note that a pledge is assumed to be a donation, not an exchange, so FASB ASU 2014-09 *Revenue from Contracts with Customers* doesn't apply.

Fundraising Events

Most nonprofit organizations conduct fundraising events to raise money for operations or specific programs. These events are usually annual fundraising events, such as mailing campaigns, marathons, golf tournaments, dinners, and galas to raise money for general use.

We have FASB Accounting Standards Codification (ASC) Document 958 that provides guidance in presenting fundraising revenues and costs on financial statements. Other pronouncements may also apply, depending on the type of event and donations.

Proceeds and expenses associated with these events are usually booked into the unrestricted/general net asset. However, if the fundraising event is for a particular program or for something to happen in the following year, then revenues from the event are considered temporarily restricted.

The difference between the amount paid and the fair value of the benefits received by the donor is recognized as a contribution, a donation.

For example, if a donor pays $200 for a dinner that is worth $150, the difference of $50 is a contribution, a "real" donation. The costs of such dinner, as benefits, are known as "Direct Donor Costs." These aren't fundraising costs; rather, they're classified as program expenses on financial statements. They could be costs of a dinner, refreshments, rent of a restaurant, etc.

Besides costs, organizations should know the fair market value (FMV) of each event and auction item, as donors may be able to deduct the difference between the amount paid and the value received in exchange. FMV is usually shown on event tickets and auction information sheets.

✓ **The direct donor benefit cost is based on actual costs, while the exchange portion is based on fair market value.**

Fundraising activities are presented in the "Statement of Activities" (Income Statement of nonprofits). Special events are shown separately along with the direct donor benefit costs associated with fundraising events. Actually, organizations may choose among three methods for recording and presenting direct benefit costs on financial statements:

o Option 1: Display the costs of direct benefits to donors as a separate line item deducted from the special event gross revenues.

o Option 2: Display gross revenues in the revenue section and the direct benefits costs as part of "other programs" or "supporting services." Allocation of the expenses may also be necessary.

o Option 3: Display both the contribution and the exchange portion as special event revenue. The benefits costs are deducted from the exchange amount.

According to the IRS, certain nonprofits need to file 990-Schedule G to give details on all gaming and fundraising activities. The schedule requires information regarding gross receipts and contributions for each event along with expenses. This schedule asks about fundraiser payments and other details.

Other considerations regarding fundraising include the following:

o Be sure the fundraising event really brings money in. Sometimes fundraisers don't account for all expenses involved in the event as many bills come in after the occasion. Nonprofits must review fundraising activities to make sure they're indeed bringing in more than they're spending. An event bringing in $100 net of all expenses may not be worth all the work.

o   Sales/Excise taxes- Each state has its own rules and laws regarding fundraising. Some states tax auctions, while other states tax all fundraising and still others offer exemptions for nonprofits. Taxes decrease revenues and, in some cases, they can be substantial.

o   If nonprofits use credit cards or third parties in fundraising, they must consider processing charges. The organization may pay 2 to 3 percent plus as a surcharge for each donation or purchase using a credit card. When budgeting for events, take into consideration these charges.

Many times organizations combine fundraising with programs or with management/general. When this happens, a reasonable allocation of expenses is applied. This situation is also known as "Joint Costs," discussed in detail in another chapter.

Nonprofits should consider FASB ASU 2014-09- *Revenue from Contracts with Customer* for fiscal years starting on December 15, 2018. Income from events is usually considered an exchange with the benefits happening at the same time as the event. In case benefits are more or happen after than just the event itself, then the situation should be analyzed to see if the revenue could be recognized right away or upon the fulfillment of the contract in the exchange.

Donation Receipts

It's always a good idea to give receipts to donors, especially when the donation is in cash. Besides being a good procedure, the IRS also has receipt requirements that nonprofits must follow.

The basic concept is that organizations should give receipts for donations over $250. As the IRS doesn't require a particular receipt form to be filled out, the receipt could be a letter, a postcard, an email message, or a form created for this purpose with the name of the organization clearly shown.

It's not necessary to add Social Security or tax ID numbers to the receipts. Per the IRS (www.irs.gov), receipts for such donations should include the following components:

- Name of organization
- Amount of cash contribution
- Description (but not the value) of non-cash contribution
- A statement that no goods or services were provided in return for the contribution if that was the case.
- Description and good-faith estimate of the value of goods or services, if any, that an organization provided in return for the contribution.
- A statement that goods or services, if any, that an organization provided in return for the contribution consisted entirely of intangible religious benefits.
- An example of such a receipt would be: "Thank you for your contribution of $450 to ABC Nonprofit made in the name of its Special Scholarship program. No goods or services were provided in exchange for your contribution."

Besides the $250 threshold, if a donor receives something in return for a contribution of $75 or more, the organization must give a receipt as well, called a "Written Disclosure." The idea is that only a part of the "donation" is a "real" donation or contribution, not the entire amount.

This statement must:

- Inform a donor that the deductible amount of the contribution for federal tax purposes is limited to the excess of money contributed by the donor over the value of goods or services provided by the organization.

- Provide a donor with a good-faith estimate of the fair market value of the goods or services.

In practice, nonprofits include this language on event tickets and other materials, making the disclosure evident and clear. It's common to see tickets for special events indicating the fair market value of the event. It seems a bit tacky, but organizations do it for a good reason.

According to the IRS, "a penalty is imposed on a charity that doesn't make the required disclosure in connection with a quid pro quo contribution of more than $75. The penalty is $10 per contribution, not to exceed $5,000 per fundraising event or mailing. The charity can avoid the penalty if it can show that the failure was due to reasonable cause."

Sometimes, organizations send annual donors' receipts by January 31 of the following year. This receipt lists all donations for the year, helping supporters file their tax returns. Computerized systems help to create these yearly statement-receipts, but this means that someone must have entered detailed data in the software, which can be time-consuming and costly but expected in some nonprofits.

Beware: People may ask for donation receipts when no donation really occurred. I've seen parents asking for donation receipts for tuition paid to a school that was part of a nonprofit. Receipts were provided for tuition, not donations. Organizations don't want to participate in tax-evasion schemes, but at the same time, they don't want to upset a member or a donor, so procedures should be in place to avoid confusion and ill feelings. Sometimes the best approach is to give people receipts with descriptions of transactions.

CEOs, presidents, or executive directors sometimes want to make the receipt more individualized and prefer to handwrite personal notes. They could use pads for receipts with the IRS information required as footers and handwrite a personal note in the blank space above. This way the donor receives a personalized thank you letter and an IRS receipt in one-step.

Save copies of receipts. Donors often lose original receipts, and the nonprofit is often expected to provide them with copies. This happens all the time, especially at tax time during March and April.

Organizations' staff should refrain from giving tax advice to donors, as the nonprofit isn't in the business of providing expert tax advice. I've seen people, including managers, telling donors that they can deduct this or that without really understanding the entire picture. A cost may be deductible on one person's tax return, but it may not be deductible on another's. Be careful here.

In-Kind Contributions- Service

Volunteers, often the soul of an organization, contribute many services—from clerical work to executive positions—giving the nonprofit culture and personality. Without volunteer work, many nonprofits would have been closed a long time ago.

How does an organization account for volunteer work? Clearly, there's a value to it, but no money changes hands. No salaries or wages are paid. FASB provide direction here, as nonprofits recognize these services if they:

- Create or enhance nonfinancial assets, and
- Are provided by individuals possessing specialized skills, and would need to be purchased if not provided by donation.

Typically, specialized skills providers include accountants, architects, doctors, electricians, nurses, plumbers, and teachers. Doctors volunteering at a summer camp for kids with disabilities would qualify for service donations. A CPA doing an organization's tax returns free of charge would qualify as well.

The basis for assigning a value to the services must be reasonable. For example, $100-$150 per hour would work for doctors or CPAs. The amount may also be the fair market value of an asset improvement resulting from the in-kind services.

✓ **Fundraising volunteers aren't recognized in the accounting books**

In most cases, donated services are booked in the unrestricted (no donor restriction) net asset. The journal entry is to debit in-kind services expense and credit in-kind services revenue. However, in some instances, due to the nature of the donation, nonprofits could capitalize the expenses, as in the case of volunteers working on building improvements, software programs, or other assets.

Keep track of volunteers with time sheets and logs. Also treat them very well as they promote the organization, providing needed services. Many nonprofits wouldn't be able to deliver the goods and services if it were not for the volunteers. Note that, details on contributed services, such as fair values and allocation methods, are parts of the "Disclosure Notes" at the end of official financial statements.

Although services may be recognized in the nonprofit's financial statements, the value of such work can't be deducted on individuals' tax returns. Donors may take a special mileage deduction and expenses related to the donated work, but they can't deduct the value of actual services, such as hourly fees. A lawyer or other professional can deduct the costs of donated paper and supplies, but not their hourly fees.

Remember to include volunteers on insurance policies. Volunteers can misbehave, steal, or fall down the stairs, and the organization is liable for these events. There are policies specifically for volunteers that should be considered.

✓ **The IRS doesn't allow the reporting of donated services, only donated goods. However, the value of such services can be added as a narrative on 990- Schedule O.**

Note that in-kind contributions, including of services, are assumed to be a donation, not an exchange, so FASB ASU 2014-09 *Revenue from Contracts with Customers* doesn't apply.

In-Kind Contributions-Donations of Things

Many people and businesses donate clothes, food, furniture, jewelry, equipment, and other items to an organization. Some even give real estate and inventory goods. However, nonprofits must be careful about what they accept as donations. For instance, a donor could donate a building and land to an organization. Should management take them? Not until building inspectors and other professionals give the property a clean bill of health or disclose any repairs or issues related to the building.

With certain real estate donations, it's possible that a significant asbestos cleanup is needed, or maybe there is a hazardous material underneath the soil, and the donation can become quite expensive to maintain.

Some large gifts may also cause unexpected increases in insurance premiums, which might be prohibitive to the organization along with too costly maintenance and fees. Due to the risks involved with large donations, usually the Executive Director and/or G&A personnel participate in making decisions about the donation of certain things. Also, policies and procedures should cover this type of contributions.

FASB ASC 820-10 (FASB 157) provides guidance on how to measure fair value consistently for goods and services. In the case of goods, the nonprofits should evaluate the products properly, following a level methodology, similar to the evaluation of investments. The levels expected to be followed if non-cash items with a value over $500 are:

- o Level 1-Item is evaluated based on quoted prices in the market for identical assets.

- o Level 2- Item is evaluated based on like-kind comparison. For example, the fair market value of a building could be derived by reviewing selling prices at various similar buildings in comparable locations.

o Level 3- Item is valued based on "unobservable" data, such as donor's estimation of fair value.

Anything of value, such as jewelry, or any goods valued at $5,000 or more should be professionally inspected, not just for insurance purposes, but for IRS compliance as well. The IRS procedures for the nonprofit are:

➢ Donor fills out Form 8283 upon donation of the gift

➢ Nonprofit management fills out Part IV of the Form 8283 upon receipt of the gift

➢ If the nonprofit sells the gift within three years, the organization files Form 8282 with a copy sent to the donor

Like in-kind services, nonprofits present in-kind goods in detail in the notes to the official financial statements, including information on the type, nature, fair market value, valuation method, and allocations of the goods.

The organization isn't usually expected to value donations for donors, and large gift valuation is usually the donor's responsibility. The nonprofit can give a receipt with a detailed description of the items donated with not much about the dollar value of the donation.

✓ **Unlike in-kind services, in-kind goods are reported on the tax return 990**.

Organizations should keep track of all in-kind goods, such as donations of furniture, computer systems, etc. Since no cash changes hands, it's easy to forget such goods, but they should be input in the accounting system as revenue and asset or expense.

Usually, in-kind contributions are unrestricted donations and not exchange. But if the donor receives something for the gift, then it may be an exchange situation and FASB ASU 2014-09- *Revenue from Contracts with Customer* may apply. For more information about this update, see the "Contribution or Exchange" section earlier in this chapter.

Donations of Art/Museum Pieces

Gifts of antiquities and works of art are a different class of contributions. These are pieces with historical or artistic value and are:

- Used for public exhibition, research, or education, as a public service and not for financial gain

- Safeguarded, protected, and cared for

- Protected by organization policy to buy more pieces for the collection, in case these items are sold

Nonprofits should evaluate the maintenance costs of museum/art objects, such climate controls, burglar alarms, cameras, security guards, and other expenses that can be substantial. So, organizations need to possess enough resources to safeguard the valuable pieces.

Existing collections and any other new gifts should be re-evaluated yearly. Some pieces could have been moved out of the organization or suffered damage. Also, insurance policies need to be updated for new items, losses, and any changes.

Nonprofits have a choice to capitalize the museum/art pieces or not. Either way, the organization needs to be consistent in dealing with the accounting for these objects. When an institution capitalizes a collection, it records it as an asset and as revenue, presenting it on a separate line item in the Statement of Financial Position (the nonprofit version of a Balance Sheet).

✓ **Capitalized collections aren't depreciated.**

Usually, museum pieces are unrestricted donations and not exchange. But if the donor receives something for the gift, then it may be an exchange situation with the FASB ASU 2014-09- *Revenue from Contracts with Customer,* covered earlier in this chapter, applying.

Split Interest Agreements

Donors could give nonprofits benefits that are shared with other parties. This type of gift, involving a split interest agreement, often includes more than one nonprofit, or a nonprofit and other parties. This setup might include a fixed payment going back to the donor until his/her death. Also, these agreements may allow for cash inflows to the organization on a long-term basis. Details are presented under the disclosure notes in financial statements.

Split interest contracts may be revocable or not. This difference is important since revocable split interest agreements are usually not recognized as revenue by the nonprofit, while irrevocable ones are. Trusts may be involved in these deals, which can be complicated. These agreements are commonly known as the following:

- o Charitable lead trusts—The nonprofit is named as beneficiary

- o Perpetual trusts held by third parties—Only income earned is distributed to the nonprofit, not the assets (corpus)that are held in trust

- o Charitable remainder trusts—When trust terms are

terminated, the nonprofit receives the remaining assets

o Charitable gift annuities—Assets are held by the organization and an annuity is set up for the third party

o Pooled (life) income funds—Investment based on life insurance policies and funding. The donor receives income until death, when the organization gets the full value of the investment

The revenue recognition issues go back to FASB ASC 820-10 (FASB 157), involving the mortality of donor and the risks involved. Revenue valuation of a split interest agreement is based on the fair market value of the asset transferred, including any liabilities. Generally, nonprofits categorize split interest agreement amounts as temporarily restricted because of the implicit time restrictions of the gift, but donor's wishes may override this classification.

Many organizations implement a "Gift Acceptance Policy" or committee" to oversee these types of gifts because they can be complex. Nonprofits should be sure the deal:

- Is legal

- Complies with the acceptable risk

- Complies with state laws and regulations

- Is the type of asset that has been approved

- Complies with the minimum gift amount

- Complies with the minimum age for immediate and deferred gifts

- Follows industry standards

- Is doable as far as gift designations are honored

Summary

Nonprofit organizations receive many types of revenues, such as cash, checks, stock donations, grants, and pledges that may or may not be collectible. Fundraising events are popular income producing activities as well. Along with regular donations, organizations may accept in-kind donations of services and things, and may be parties to split interest agreements. Revenues can be classified several ways as they may be restricted or not, and may be recognized as contributions or exchanges. FASB ASU 2014-09 has specific requirements for exchanges.

Not all revenues are the same, even though they seem similar. Besides IRS receipting rules, nonprofit management needs to analyze the types and restrictions to classify the funds properly in the financial statements and tax forms.

6 - Government Grants

"The object of government in peace and in war is not the glory of rulers or of races, but the happiness of the common man."

Lord William Beveridge (1879-1963)

T he government's job is about governing, protecting, and helping people as the saying above indicates. However, governments are too large to provide certain services to many communities. This weakness is where nonprofits shine, as they can provide services governments cannot deliver as well and as efficiently.

The government gives grants to nonprofits so they can offer goods and services to a community. Such awards often involve large sums of money, and, not surprisingly, grantors want assurances that nonprofits will spend the funds properly. These awards can come from the state, city, county, or federal sources. In this chapter, we will concentrate on federal U.S. grants.

Governmental awards include their own language, rules, and reporting requirements, which can be complex. For instance, some awards pay organizations ahead of time, while others require filing reports before funds are released for reimbursement. Also, some grants pay nonprofits based on headcount and not on expenses incurred.

✓ **Grants aren't repaid. They're payments for goods and services provided.**

A comprehensive listing of government grants is available in the Catalog of Federal Financial Assistance (CFDA) at https://www.cfda.gov/. This catalog lists all available federal grants and is updated often. The number of federal grants given by top agencies in July 2017 was:

519 Department of Health and Human Services

289 Department of the Interior

270 Department of Agriculture

145 Department of Justice

115 Department of Housing and Urban Development

This CFDA website allows many ways to look for grants: by keyword, agency, beneficiary type, etc. Each grant has a specific number and purpose, allowing development staff to search for grants available, requirements and information about the application process. Another good website about federal government grants is www.grants.gov. It contains links to grants, help in writing grant proposals, and useful resources.

Once a grant is awarded, the nonprofit can register and access the "System for Award Management" (SAM) that consolidates many rules and functions. This system is at https://www.sam.gov.

Many nonprofits function as "pass-through" entities to other parties. For instance, an organization receives funds for research and then distributes them to appropriate institutions. The organization doesn't do the research but gives the money to others involved with particular research interests.

It's essential for organizations with pass-through funds to get enough money to manage the grants coming in and going out. Not all money is pass-through; some funds must stay within the organization to cover direct and indirect costs associated with the management of such grants.

Sometimes government entities make nonprofits the intermediary, inadvertently. A real-life example: A school used to receive state checks to distribute to disabled students every month. The government agency should have mailed the checks to the families' addresses, but instead, it sent the money to the school. The situation created an administrative burden for the school, which was not getting anything for this work. When the school started to return the checks, the agency began to send the money directly to the families. The point of this vignette: Organizations should not do free work for the government.

An interesting byproduct of a nonprofit funded by various government agencies is that their accountants become specialists in each grant because of the complexity involved in each contract, including specific reporting and different ways to obtain funds. Compliance issues, deadlines, and matters related to each grant reporting can be different.

This specialization can help accountants get jobs in other nonprofits or businesses that receive the same type of funding. As expected, staff with the right grant expertize can be precious and popular with many organizations.

Financial Management

As of December 2014, nonprofits must comply with a "Super OMB Circular," also known as the "Omni Circular." Its official name is "OMB Uniform Guidance: Administrative Requirements, Cost Principles, and Audit Requirements for Federal Awards." This guidance will replace a few circulars, such as A-110, A-122, and A-133, streamlining the process of acquiring and maintaining federal grants while trying to avoid duplication and waste. You can check this guideline out at https://www.ecfr.gov/cgi-bin/text-idx?tpl=/ecfrbrowse/Title02/2cfr200_main_02.tpl

The Omni Circular also specifies the information required from federal agencies when announcing funding opportunities and evaluating nonprofits as recipients. Some issues government agencies need to consider would be:

- Organization financial stability
- Quality of management and systems
- Audit reports
- Performance history

If a nonprofit is deemed risky, it most likely will get a grant based on reimbursement of costs instead of advance funding.

Many organizations prepare summary worksheets or tables on each contract with specific details regarding requirements, reports, dates, etc. to manage grand deadlines and compliance issues. Instead of going through an entire document to find an item, one could go to the summary, saving lots of time and effort. Nonprofits may also create a calendar listing the deadlines for each grant contract. They may employ computerized reminders to send out emails reminding managers of upcoming deadlines and other compliance issues that can cost nonprofits a lot of money.

The primary information source for federal grants, the Super or Omni Circular, is clear about the financial expectations for grantees, including requirements such as:

> ➤ The ability to identify each grant received and expenses associated with each grant

> ➤ The resources to provide accurate, current, and complete financial reporting as required

> ➤ The maintenance of proper records

> ➤ Appropriate internal controls

> ➤ Written procedures for allowable costs and grant payments

> ➤ Comparison of expenditures with budget amounts for each federal award

---

If a nonprofit isn't on the accrual basis, but the granting agency requires accrual reporting, the organization doesn't need to convert its accounting books to accrual, only the grant reports. This conversion can be done by adjusting the report numbers only.

Federal grantors want organizations to spend federal money right away with reimbursement as the preferred funding method. This means that nonprofits first spend the money and then request "drawdowns" as reimbursements.

When an organization receives more than $120,000 in federal money, it should deposit the money in insured, preferably interest-bearing, bank accounts. The government doesn't want its money deposited in risky financial institutions.

Note that if nonprofits earn interest of $500 or less, they can use the money to defray costs. However, in case the interest is more than $500, they must send the funds to the grantor. Check your grant agreement carefully regarding this topic. The idea here is to minimize the chances of losses and waste.

Funding Cuts or Delays

Funding cuts and delays are serious issues for nonprofits. To minimize this problem, nonprofits should file online reports promptly and with no errors. Grant payments may also be held back when the required reports about program results and costs aren't provided, or when they are incomplete.

✓ **Organizations should apply for lines of credit before they need them.**

Another issue organizations must deal with is the risk of funding cuts due to government budgets constraints and cuts. Therefore, nonprofits must have a "Plan B" that may involve cuts in administration, programs, or fundraising costs. Maybe some people could work part-time instead of full time, for example.

A significant risk involved with grants is the noncompliance with terms of the agreement. I worked in a medical-related nonprofit where the therapist employed didn't have all the education and experience required for the position, as required in the contract. The organization had a $100,000 reduction of its grant for the following year, which was material, forcing it to eliminate another program to absorb the cut.

All individuals involved in a government-funded program, not just finance personnel, should know the particulars of the contract, including required details about personnel education and experience. It's a good idea for the human resources department to learn of these issues along with program managers.

If cuts or delays happen, cash management should come into play. Some bills may wait, while others, such as payroll, must be paid in a timely fashion. Some organizations use proceeds from program fees or special events to cover these liabilities. Others utilize bank lines of credit to provide the required cash flow and remain afloat. Nonprofits should always have a cushion to absorb unexpected budget cuts or delays.

Grant Budgets

Usually, nonprofits' grant proposals include budget numbers that are carefully considered, showing a realistic cost plan for the organization. These numbers are classified as direct and indirect and may be negotiated with the federal agency.

Budgets are parts of a grant contract and can be for one or more years. However, errors can happen, and unexpected things can happen such as major changes in the scope of services, calling for alterations in the budget numbers. Such changes may be allowed, depending on grantor and situation.

Grant budget line items may also include some flexibility. If a budget has five lines within the administrative section, for instance, the total of such expenses may be considered, not each line. Suppose a nonprofit has an expense of $50 in postage-Administration to be reimbursed by a grant. However, the organization had spent all the postage line item in the budget. Depending on the contract, this postage cost may be applied to a supplies line item.

Many grantors provide templates and other assistance in developing budgets, but narratives and explanations are also part of the budget process—not just numbers. Often, the accounting department must work with programs to assemble a report that meets both the quantitative and description sections.

When nonprofits have grants, the process of recognizing expenses is more complicated, involving not only regular accounting classifications but also identification of grants covering such expenses.

Nonprofits must implement financial systems that segregate revenues and expenses by grant, so that the individual reports can be generated easily. To this end, a grant module may be utilized. Unlike regular accounting software, this module doesn't close every year, offering a layer of flexibility to the process. Some modules allow for notes, comments and can even help in the calculation and application of overhead, saving a lot of time.

When nonprofits employ such software, their staff must enter each revenue and expense with the regular accounts plus a grant module code. This process can improve reporting and management of awards, but it may increase the workload in the finance department, with some delays in processing accounts payable.

For example, if a nonprofit receives a bill for supplies, the staff needs to know not only the proper expense account but also the program and grant classification. This is particularly important when a program is funded by more than one grant. Because of the module cost and extra-work required with complex grant modules, usually only large organizations employ those.

Cost Principles

The federal grant cost principles are similar to the GAAP cost principles, but they aren't the same. While administrative costs are typically indirect costs, the idea of "allowable" costs doesn't exist with GAAP. Another difference is in vocabulary. For example, the word "cost" is used in grants, but the word "expense" is traditionally used with GAAP.

Total costs of a federal grant comprise the following:

➢ Allowable direct costs plus

➢ Allowable indirect costs plus or minus

➢ Applicable credits

For costs to be allowed, they must be reasonable, consistent, documented, and mostly follow GAAP in accounting treatment. Not all costs are allowed in federally funded programs, and organizations must employ common sense and fairness in spending federal grants. For instance, purchases of luxury goods are unnecessary and make no sense, especially when there are cheaper alternatives. Buying $200 wine bottles for the homeless is likely not to be allowable.

Allowable costs should be "allocable" to the program, i.e., the costs must be connected to the program, directly or indirectly. For example, if the executive director goes on a cruise for a vacation, federal grants may not cover its costs. Entertainment costs aren't allowable unless they're part of programs or were pre-approved or authorized in the budget. However, provisions exist to cover childcare, in an effort for federal grant recipients to be more "family-friendly." Therefore, nonprofits must review grant contract costs carefully.

According to many grant contracts, organizations can't use vendors that aren't permitted to participate in federally funded programs. The government keeps a list of companies that can't be used for grant-funded projects at www.sam.gov. If a nonprofit employs any of them, the costs aren't reimbursed.

States and even cities may have different vendors that are banned from government contracts, so inquire about those and their effects on federal grants.

Besides allowable costs, grant contracts mention credits, which could be discounts, insurance refunds, or error corrections decreasing costs. For instance, if a nonprofit receives a $100 rebate on a purchase using federal funding, the $100 should be netted against grant costs, decreasing them.

More than one grant may fund costs, making it necessary to allocate costs correctly to each funding source. Typically, one grant can't cover another grant's deficiency, unless it's pre-approved. "Double-dipping," i.e., receiving funds for the same expense from difference sources, isn't acceptable.

Indirect costs are usually identified and reimbursed as part of a plan and a rate. An organization may submit a "Cost Allocation Plan" (CAP) identifying direct and indirect costs when applying for government grants and/or to arrive at a reasonable indirect cost rate. It can also be employed when a nonprofit is new, or if it plans to start a new program. See an excerpt of this report next- available at the Department of Interior website https://www.doi.gov/ibc/services/Indirect_Cost_Services/upload/Sample-Cost-Allocation-Plan-State-2.doc .

Schedule B			DIRECT PROGRAMS and ACTIVITIES (6/30/xx)					
A	B	C	D	E	F	G	H	I
ELEMENTS OF COSTS	FINANCIAL STATEMENT EXPENDITURES	ADJUSTMENTS/ UNALLOWABLE COSTS	ENVIRONMENTAL SERVICES	HEAD START & OTHERS	WEATHERI- ZATION	FUNDRAISING	(D)+(E)+(F)+(G) TOTAL DIRECT COSTS	INDIRECT COSTS
Salaries and wages	$1,327,638	0	$140,831	$950,615	$18,305	$1,592	$1,111,343	$216,295
Fringe benefits	$245,434	0	$28,138	$170,107	$3,657	$317	$202,219	$43,215
Subtotal labor & fringes	$1,573,072	0	$168,969	$1,120,722	$21,962	$1,909	$1,313,562	$259,510
Contractual services	$245,420	0	$3,493	$207,770	$34,157	$0	$245,420	$0
Depreciation/use allowance	$41,582	0	$0	$0	$0	$0	$0	$41,582
Emergency asst. payments	$72,859	0	$52,809	$0	$20,050	$0	$72,859	$0
Equipment rental and maintenance	$11,448	0	$592	$5,197	$0	$281	$6,070	$5,378
Equipment / capital	$58,215	($58,215)	$0	$0	$0	$0	$0	$0
Equipment / minor	$546	0	$0	$0	$546	$0	$546	$0
Program materials	$124,616	0	$0	$124,616	$0	$0	$124,616	$0
Insurance	$12,554	0	$92	$8,209	$85	$373	$8,759	$3,795
Occupancy	$129,314	0	$24,637	$100,956	$459	$233	$126,285	$3,029
Office supplies	$32,540	0	$1,794	$13,317	$3,649	$842	$19,602	$12,938

When certain costs are unusual or if questions arise on the appropriateness and allocation of certain expenses, nonprofits should negotiate with the government in advance whenever possible. The situation is the same with consolidations and other exemptions—all need approvals by a federal agency, and the sooner, the better. If an organization has questionable costs, it may not be reimbursed for these expenses. Better be safe than sorry.

Sometimes GAAP conflicts with grant accounting, such as in accounting for certain leases, where per GAAP the amounts should be capitalized, but if that happens, the organization may not be reimbursed according to some grant agreements. In these situations, most nonprofits keep the internal accounting according to GAAP, and, in a worksheet, adjust the numbers to comply with grant reimbursement rules. This way the organization can be repaid for what it's due, while keeping backup documentation, in the case of any questions.

Also, note that GAAP requires an expense allocation by natural and functional areas often shown on the Schedule of Functional Expenses. This allocation can be different from the one acceptable for grants.

Direct and Indirect Costs

Direct costs

Direct costs are those readily identified with a particular program, as nonprofits can assign these costs to a specific activity with great accuracy. Examples would be art supplies for an art program, art teachers who work only in one program, and mailing costs particular to the program.

Direct costs are often related to salaries of individuals working in particular programs. To capture this data, nonprofits often use time sheets to identify people working on specific projects. Employees fill out online or paper time sheets that may be pre-coded for the work they currently perform. These numbers along with pay rates are transferred to the accounting system, separating each employee's pay to the proper program and grant. For example, salaries for people working in the art program will show up in different grant reports from the ones working in childcare. Such data should be reviewed by supervisors to identify and correct any errors.

✓ **Costs should be real, no estimated or budgeted amounts.**

Indirect Costs

Also known as overhead, these costs can't be assigned to a program or funding source directly. Indirect costs must be related to the project grant, but can't be readily identified. This can be similar to the GAAP indirect rate, but it's not exactly the same because grants may exclude some items and may have its own unique requirements. The Super Circular explains this area in detail.

✓ **State and another government grantor may also define and calculate indirect costs differently.**

Unlike direct cost payments, the government pays indirect costs based on a percentage, which could be applied towards total direct costs (see Indirect Cost Rates section). If an organization reports $1,000 in direct expense, then, depending on the situation, 20 percent may be added to reflect overhead costs and the nonprofit would be paid $1,200.

The Omni or Super Circular allows for a standard 10 percent indirect/overhead rate for all organizations receiving federal funds. This standard rate is set indefinitely without annual approvals. The percentage is applied to modified total direct costs (MTDC), which includes all direct salaries and wages, appropriate fringe benefits, materials and supplies, services, travel, and sub-awards/subcontracts, up to $25,000 for each one. MTDC excludes the following:

- Equipment (items over $5,000)

- Capital expenditures

- Charges for patient care

- Rental costs

- Tuition remission

- Scholarships

- Fellowships

- Participant support costs

- Sub-awards and sub-contracts in excess of the first $25,000

Note that the incentive is to show high MTDC to get a larger base for the set percentage. For example, 10 percent of an MTDC of $15,000 is greater than 10 percent of MTDC of $11,000. The larger the MTDC, the better off the organization will be. Because of this situation, nonprofits may change the way some costs are derived so they can be classified as direct. For example, institutions may give passwords to copy machine users to allocate copy expenses directly to individual projects.

Organizations can still negotiate rates with the government, especially large ones that implement rates much higher than 10 percent. I've seen an indirect rate of 88 percent, so there is room for negotiations.

A summary of direct and indirect costs:

	Direct Costs	Indirect Costs
Characteristics	Easy to allocate to a program	Hard to allocate to a specific program
Grant funding	Paid based on actual direct costs	Paid based on an approved percentage or the standard 10%

Indirect Cost Rates

As indirect cost rates can be substantial, many nonprofits negotiate with a government agency to increase their rates. As mentioned before, the 10 percent default rate based on the Super Circular isn't likely to work with large entities, and many will need to negotiate higher rates.

For an indirect cost rate to be approved by a federal agency, the nonprofit must submit a worksheet showing all expenses classified as direct or indirect and unallowable costs. This could be a CAP or other document showing past performance to estimate reasonableness for the rate.

The most popular method to allocate indirect costs is based on direct salaries, but many organizations have total costs as the basis for calculations. Once approved indirect cost rates may be extended up to four years without rate negotiations, subject to approval by the federal agency.

The idea is to be reasonable in allocating indirect costs. Some accepted ways to derive the indirect cost rate and do the allocations are:

- o Simplified - All programs benefit from indirect costs to about the same degree. The idea is to implement one rate and go with it. This method is often used by small organizations that don't receive many federal grants.

- o Multiple - Indirect costs benefit a nonprofit organization's major functions in varying degrees. They accumulate in separate pools that hold similar characteristics and functions. Instead of calculating one rate, the organization gets multiple rates.

- o Special - Sometimes, factors preclude nonprofits from employing either the simplified or the multiple allocation types. Maybe the nature of the nonprofit work doesn't allow for such allocations. Alternatively, certain issues, such as the physical site of the work, would not permit the usage of the other methods. The organization then may consider the special rate.

Once the rate is set, staff needs to input only direct costs in the Internet-based reporting system of the federal government—the software applies the proper rate. If $300 is entered for reimbursement with an indirect rate of 50 percent, the nonprofit will be reimbursed $450. The larger the organization, generally the larger the indirect cost rate.

Is the rate really covering all indirect costs? To verify the reasonableness of calculations of indirect cost rates, management should compare grant money received to the actual indirect expenses. Depending on the difference, the organization may need to change the rate in the future.

As the process and calculations for indirect cost rates can be complicated and detailed, many government agencies provide specific guidance, such as the U.S. Department of Agriculture (USDA) that conducts webinars and provides other assistance, according to its website at http://nifa.usda.gov/business/indirect_cost_process.html.

Other government websites also disseminate information and give examples of indirect cost rate process, format and information required. You can check them out at:

http://www.epa.gov/ogd/recipient/sample1.htm

http://www.doi.gov/ibc/services/indirect_cost_services/FAQs.cfm

---

Grant Audit

As expected, the federal government is concerned that the grants are spent properly, requiring audits of nonprofit recipients in addition to regular visits from the federal agency staff.

Instead of having a separate audit of each major grant, the Single Audit allows for one independent audit covering all federal grant contracts. It usually combines an audit of the organization and its grants. According to the National Council of Nonprofits, "a single audit covers the entire scope of the organization's financial operations, ensuring that:

- The financial statements are presented fairly;

- The organization has an adequate internal control structure, and that

- The organization is in compliance with any special government regulations/laws that apply to the specific type of federal funding the audit covers."

These single audits are required if the nonprofit has spent $750,000 or more in federal funds (This threshold is likely to change in the future). Single audits are performed by independent CPA firms, which usually carry out both regular and single audits within the same engagement, releasing the results in two different reports—one for the regular portion and another for the grant audit.

When an auditor prepares the cost allocation plan or indirect cost proposal, he/she can't do the grant audit if the indirect cost recovered is over $1 million in the prior year.

During a single audit, a CPA firm evaluates the fairness of the financial statements and the schedule of federal financial assistance, which contains information about grants. To this end, auditors assess risk by reviewing prior findings, internal controls, and usage of contractors. Also, CPA personnel should consider the materiality of the funds, with major grants often getting most of the attention.

The Super Circular clarifies that auditors are responsible for following up on any deficiencies, also called "findings." The nonprofit is supposed to respond with a corrective action plan. All of these documents are forwarded to the appropriate government agency.

Management should be aware of the cumulative grant spending because as the organization gets closer to the $750,000 in annual grant expenses, it should start budgeting for the single audit. It doesn't come cheap, and grant funds may have to be adjusted to include this cost.

Note that nonprofits may need to have a regular, less detailed audit to comply with grantor or state rules. For example, the states of Connecticut and Hawaii require the filing of audited financial statements of charities with an annual gross income of $500,000 or more regardless of federal funding. This audit is less detailed and cheaper than the Single Audit, but it needs to be done.

Other Grant Considerations

Federal grant contracts contain many details that warrant some attention since they may seem odd to readers not familiar with grant compliance. Some issues to consider are:

Standard of Conduct

Nonprofits must implement written standards of conduct related to conflicts of interest and behavior of employees involved in the selection, award, and administration of grants. The government wants to avoid a situation where organizations utilize mostly businesses owned by board members, for example.

Computers

Computer devices with costs under the nonprofit's capitalization policy or $5,000 are considered personal property at the same level as supplies. This rule decreased prior compliance requirements when computers were classified as equipment.

Royalties

The nonprofit may copyright federally funded work; however, the government reserves a royalty-free, nonexclusive, and irrevocable right to reproduce, publish, or otherwise use the work for federal purposes, including authorizing others to do so.

Bid

Fair competition and other requirements are required for federally funded purchases, except for micro purchases, typically $3,000 or less.

Sharing Information

The idea is for government agencies to share information and to analyze reports to improve programs and services across the board, spreading adoptions of practices that worked well for individual organizations.

Mandatory Disclosures

Nonprofits must disclose all violations of federal criminal law involving bribery, fraud, or gratuity violations that can potentially affect the federal award. Note that disclosures for grants are different from disclosures for financial statements.

Grant Resources

Next are some helpful websites regarding grants:

Reconnecting America -- http://reconnectingamerica.org/resource-center/federal-grant-opportunities/

US Government Grants and Loans -- https://www.usa.gov/grants

Grant Watch -- https://www.grantwatch.com/resources.php

Summary

Nonprofits receiving government grants to fund programs and operations must follow the guidelines in the Super or Omni Circular, the federal government publication that unified old circulars. It specifies a standard 10 percent indirect cost rate and clarifies certain classifications.

Organizations must recognize direct and indirect costs related to each grant program to be able to obtain a non-standard indirect cost rate after submitting a Cost Allocation Plan and other documentation to the proper federal agency.

7 - Financial Statements

"I know at last what distinguishes man from animals: financial worries."

Romain Rolland, French Writer, (1866-1944)

Nonprofits don't have owners per se, but they have many interested parties who are concerned about the organizations financial well-being. Stakeholders such as managers and boards of directors are attentive to financial matters to run the organization properly, while grantors may be more interested in economic issues involving grants.

Management and the board of directors typically get financial reports that don't need to follow the "Generally Accepted Accounting Principles" – GAAP but must be reliable enough to help manage operations. These internal reports often compare actual numbers to budgets, helping managers in making better decisions.

119

While internal users use these budget reports, external users may prefer to receive GAAP-based financial statements because they're consistent and comparable to other nonprofits' reports. The GAAP statements must follow strict rules, making them the preferred format for many users, including bankers and grantors.

Various readers of GAAP "official" statements, such as prospective or current donors, may look for issues that prevent the nonprofit from maintaining existing programs or other serious financial problems. If a supporter sees administrative expenses increasing while programs expenses are decreasing, it could raise some concerns. Maybe the organization is cutting down on programs. This trend may also be a sign that management is planning an expansion, hiring administrative personnel first; the situation may be temporary.

✓ **Financial statements include notes and disclosures to clarify the numbers on the reports.**

This chapter covers reporting according to GAAP, as per FASB Document ASC-958, specific to nonprofits and other pronouncements. In the past, organizations followed SFAS 117 *Financial Statements of Not-for-Profit Organizations,* but this report is now a part of FASB Accounting Standards Codification (ASC).

We also discuss issues related to the FASB Accounting Standards Update- ASU 2016-14 *Presentation of Financial Statements of Not-for-Profit Entities* that changes the presentation of financial statements effective in 2018 for most organizations. This update alters the net assets, requires more information on certain expenses, and involves more disclosures focusing on the liquidity of the organization.

Standard "official" financial reports contain some similarities with for-profit reporting. They are:

- **The Statement of Financial Position** - similar to the for-profit's Balance Sheet. It includes information on cash, receivables and net assets balances.

- **The Statement of Activities** - similar to the for-profit's Income Statement. Revenues and expenses are presented with expenses often in summary form.

- **The Statement of Cash Flows** - similar to the for-profit's Cash Flow Statement (ASC 230 is a guideline specific to this report).

- **The Statement of Functional Expenses** - unique nonprofit report, showing details of expenditures. Required of more organizations according to the ASU 2016-24.

We will be covering each of these statements next.

Statement of Financial Position

The Statement of Financial Position follows the formula:

Assets= Liabilities + Net Assets

This statement is similar to a for-profit company's balance sheet. The main difference is that instead of presenting "Retained Earnings," this report shows "Net Assets."

The Statement of Financial Position typically provides information on all net assets, which can also be detailed in notes of financial statements. We have a few formats allowed by ASC 958-205 and 210, but we will be covering the most common and traditional presentation methods here.

As with the balance sheet, the focus of the Statement of Financial Position is to present the liquidity of an organization — it shows cash balances, payables, and receivables. For instance, if a supporter wants to donate $1 million to a charity, but sees $1,000 in cash, $2,000 in receivables, and over $100,000 in payables, this person may wonder how the organization will pay this massive liability and may not donate to the nonprofit.

The sequence of the elements presented in this statement is based on liquidity, with the most liquid asset—cash—shown first, followed by current receivables. Liabilities are also displayed based on those that are due first, followed by longer-term obligations. It's no surprise that banks often use this statement to assess a nonprofit's cash situation and its ability to pay back loans.

Nonprofits present the Statement of Financial Position in various ways with the examples of the most popular styles, summary, and classified versions, shown next. Note that reports showing two consecutive years are standard with many organizations.

Summary version after ASU2016-14:

Do Good Organization
Statements of Financial Position
Dec. 31, 20X2 and 20X1

	20x2	20x1
Assets		
Cash and cash equivalents	xxx	xxx
Grant receivable	xxx	xxx
Prepaid expenses	xxx	xxx
Property and equipment	xxx	xxx
Total Assets	**xxx**	**xxx**
Liabilities		
Accounts payable	xxx	xxx
Deposits	xxx	xxx
Total Liabilities	**xxx**	**xxx**
Net Assets		
Net Assets Without Donor Restrictions	xxx	xxx
Net Assets With Donor Restrictions	xxx	xxx
Total Net Assets	**xxx**	**xxx**
Total Liabilities and Net Assets	xxx	xxx

Classified statement version- one year only - after ASU 2016-14:

Do Good Organization
Statement of Financial Position
Dec. 31, 20X2

Assets	
Current Assets:	
Cash and cash equivalents	xxx
Short term investments	xxx
Grants receivable	xxx
Contributions receivable	
Without donor restrictions	xxx
With donor restrictions	xxx
Total contribution receivable	xxx
Accounts receivable	xxx
Prepaid expenses	xxx
Total current assets	**xxx**
Property and equipment	xxx
Total Assets	**xxx**
Liabilities	
Current liabilities:	xxx
Accounts payable	xxx
Accrued expenses	xxx
Total current liabilities	**xxx**
Total liabilities	**xxx**
Net assets	
Without Donor Restrictions	xxx
With Donor Restrictions	xxx
Total Net Assets	**xxx**
Total Liabilities and Net Assets	**xxx**

The classified style is preferable after ASU 2016-14 since it helps in verifying liquidity—what balances are current and what aren't . Next are some interesting components of the Statement of Financial Position to be considered:

Cash and Cash Equivalents: This includes currency, petty cash, savings, and liquid, secure securities, such as U.S. Treasury bills.

Be careful with the cash balance number at year-end. I know of a too-aggressive accountant who moved funds from cash-bank accounts to investments, forgetting about outstanding checks. The result was an odd, negative cash balance at year-end.

Pledges or Grants Receivable: Commitments to donate shown at net realizable value—the amount the organization expects to receive. This number may be discounted and be net of an allowance for uncollectible pledges.

Prepaid Expenses: Amounts paid in advance that will become "real" expenses, as time passes. Usual examples are insurance payments and prepaid rent.

Investments: Stocks, bonds, and other investments evaluated following GAAP accounting rules.

Fixed Assets or Property, Plant, and Equipment: This line reflects the net book value of fixed assets—original cost less accumulated depreciation.

Organizations used to expense all fixed assets and not capitalize them. After 1994, nonprofits started to capitalize, as they were given the choice to do so. Therefore, financial statements may show odd numbers for assets -- some capitalized and some not.

Accounts Payable: Amounts owed to vendors. Unpaid salaries, taxes, or other significant liabilities may be reported separately.

Grants Payable: Promises made to individuals, businesses or other nonprofits.

Refundable Advances: These are also known as "Deposits" or "Deferred Revenue." They're amounts (not donations) received that belong to the future. For example, this might be a fee for a course scheduled in the following fiscal year.

Long-Term Debt: Principal and interest owed to creditors. The debt could be a bank loan, bond, or private debt financing.

Net Assets:

Net Assets Without Donor Restrictions – Unrestricted net assets, including board-directed limitations that must be disclosed in the notes to official financial statements. Used for daily activities.

Net Assets With Donor Restrictions – Made up of temporarily restricted net assets and endowments, also known as permanently restricted net assets.

I've witnessed instances where the board reviews only the Statement of Activities or a listing of income and expenses compared to budget amounts. They don't consider the Statement of Position, so, directors have no idea how much cash or receivables the nonprofit has, valuable information to review when making decisions. So, boards should evaluate the Statement of Position, where the cash, receivables, and liabilities are listed, not just budget reports.

Statement of Activities

The Statement of Activities follows the formula:

> **Revenues - Expenses = Change in Net Assets + Beginning Net Asset Balance = Ending Net Asset Balance**

This report, the "Income Statement" of nonprofits, presents revenues and expenses during a period of time. However, instead of showing a net income or loss at the bottom, it shows a "Change in net assets," "Increase in Net Assets" or a "Decrease in Net Assets." Then two lines follow, "Net assets at the Beginning of the Year" and "Net Assets at the End of the Year."

✓ **The term "Change in Net Assets" is equivalent to the "Net Income or Loss" from the for-profit world.**

One of the major differences between the for-profit income statement and the nonprofit version is the net asset classification, often presented in columns, giving the Statement of Activities a matrix-like appearance. Columns are labeled according to each type of net asset-- Net Assets Without Donor Restrictions and With Donor Restrictions. Before ASU 2016-14, there were three columns – Unrestricted, temporarily restricted and permanently restricted net assets. After ASU 2016-14, the two restricted net assets are combined into one column called Net Assets With Donor Restrictions.

You can see next an example of the Statement of Activities showing the net assets in separate columns, a typical presentation. Some organizations prefer to report specific natural and functional expenses here, but usually these details are presented in a different place.

Do Very Good Organization
Statement of Activities
As of December 31, 20XX

	Net Assets Without Donor Restrictions	Net Assets With Donor Restrictions	Total
REVENUES			
Contributions	3,050	6,000	9,050
Fundraising activities	500	300	800
Professional programs	100		100
Net assets released	300	(300)	
TOTAL REVENUES	**3,950**	**6,000**	**9,950**
EXPENSES			
Programs:			
Program A	350		350
Program B	220		220
Program C	150		150
Management and General	500		500
Fundraising	100		100
TOTAL EXPENSES	**1,320**		**1,320**
Change in net assets	2,630	6,000	8,630
Net Assets at beg. of year	2,500	500	3,000
Net Assets at end of year	**5,130**	**6,500**	**11,630**

Details of some components of this statement:

Contributions: Donations and gifts made by individuals or businesses, but not government grants (grants are presented separately).

Fundraising Activities: Revenues originated from development activities, such as campaigns.

Professional Programs: Fees and any other income received from programs.

Expenses: All expenses are shown as unrestricted, as expected. They're listed by program, management & general, and fundraising. Expenses need to be reported in both natural and functional forms according to the ASU 2016-14. So, in this case, another statement showing individual items needs to be provided, most likely the "Statement of Functional Expenses."

Net Assets Released from Restrictions: Temporarily restricted revenue/net assets used during the current period. In this case, $300 was "moved" to the unrestricted net asset, resulting in a zero net effect overall.

Net Assets at the Beginning of the Year: Ending balance of the prior year brought forward.

Net Assets at the End of the Year: Beginning balance plus/minus changes in net assets. These numbers flow into the "Statement of Financial Position."

Note that under ASU 2016-14, investment expenses are to be netted against investment income. Also, underwater endowments decreases are shown as part of the restricted net asset, not unrestricted, as it has been the case earlier.

I've reviewed Statements of Activities and tax returns that show no fundraising expenses, which is odd. Most nonprofits typically present something under fundraising, such as postage or phone expenditures. The absence of a reasonable amount for fundraising raises the possibility of errors. Usually, program area has the most expenses followed by administration and then fundraising.

Statement of Cash Flows

The Statement of Cash Flows follows the formula:

Cash from Operations + from Investing + from Financing = Net increase/decrease in cash and cash equivalents + Beginning cash and cash equivalents = Cash and cash equivalents at the end of the year

This report is very similar to the for-profit cash flow statement. It shows where the cash came from and where it was spent. This report assists management, donors, and creditors in the following:

o Capacity to create positive cash flows in the future by analyzing history.

o Ability to pay program obligations and other financial obligations by analyzing cash flows.

o Evaluation of the differences between "Net assets increases/decreases" and cash receipts and payments.

o Assessment of details of cash and non-cash items, details of investments, and other financial l transactions.

Per ASC 948-230, the Statement of Cash Flows is required as part of a nonprofit's financial statements set. It complements the other two financial reports, showing cash transactions not available on any other statement. As with the for-profit cash flow statement, this one shows cash flows in three categories:

Operating Activities: Contain all activities not related to investing or financing like receipts for general contributions. This section Includes day-to-day cash activities, such as rent and supply payments along with unrestricted revenues.

Investing Activities: Display cash flows related to purchases and sales of investments, such as of plant and equipment.

Financing Activities: Show the acquisition and repayment of capital, such as loans and payments. It also contains donations restricted for long-term purposes, such as cash received as an endowment.

The operating activities portion of this statement can be prepared using the direct or indirect method.

- ✓ The direct method specifies what the cash transactions were for, such as supplies or salaries.

- ✓ The indirect method shows increases and decreases in accounts, such as receivables or payable accounts.

The direct method is easier to understand and evaluate, while the indirect method is easier to compile, making it the preferred method for many organizations. FASB recommends the direct method but still recognizes the indirect one (After ASU 2016-14, there is no longer the need to reconcile the direct method numbers to the indirect method).

It's important to note that the "Cash Flow Statement" or "Statement of Cash Flows" may mean different things to different people. Often, a budget report showing projected cash inflows and outflows is also called a Cash Flow Statement, creating some confusion. Make sure you understand what is presented.

You can see next an example of a Statement of Cash Flows using the indirect method, the one used by most nonprofits:

Habitat House, Inc.
Statement of Cash Flows
Year Ended June 30, 20X7

CASH FLOWS FROM OPERATING ACTIVITIES

Increase in net assets	200,000
Adjustments to reconcile increase in net asset with cash	
Depreciation	5,000
Increase in accounts payable	300
Increase in payroll tax liabilities	400
NET CASH PROVIDED BY OPERATING ACTIVITIES	**205,700**

CASH FLOWS FROM IN INVESTING ACTIVITIES

Purchase of new equipment	(5,000)
Short term investment-net	(1,000)
NET CASH FLOWS USED IN INVESTING ACTIVITIES	**(6,000)**

CASH FLOWS FROM FINANCING ACTIVITIES

Collection on restricted contribution for long term purposes:	
Capital Campaign	10,000
New men's shelter	2,000
Payments on loan	(500)
NET CASH PROVIDED BY FINANCING ACTIVITIES	**11,500**
NET INCREASE IN CASH AND CASH EQUIVALENTS	211,200
BEGINNING CASH AND CASH EQUIVALENTS	50,000
ENDING CASH AND CASH EQUIVALENTS	261,200

This report reconciles the cash balance to the change in net assets. It answers the question about how cash transactions contributed to the change. In this example, we see that depreciation was added back to the increase in net assets (net income in the for-profit world). This is because depreciation isn't a cash transaction, but it decreases the net assets. Therefore, it should be added back to the net assets to get the proper cash flows.

As expected, this example shows restricted long-term donations, such as funds from a Capital Campaign, as financing activities. The increase in net assets should agree with the change in the Statement of Activities; the ending cash and cash equivalents would agree with the cash balance in the Statement of Position.

One of the issues of the Statement of Cash Flows is the ability to compile the proper information. Even when created on a computer, this report may contain errors. Usually, the Statements of Position are analyzed for two consecutive years to get the numbers for operating activities.

Banks are interested in this statement. If a nonprofit wants to increase its line of credit or obtain more loans, bank loan managers are likely to review this report for clues about the risks of giving the organization more credit. But note that more often than not, banks would like to see more details of cash flows, including their timing, not available in this report.

Statement of Functional Expenses

The Statement of Functional Expenses follows the formula:

Program Expenses + Administrative Expenses + Fundraising Expenses = Total Expenses

---

This statement is typical of nonprofit organizations and has no real counterpart in the for-profit world. By analyzing expenses, the report helps users determine how effectively an organization is fulfilling its mission and using its resources. This statement can also be utilized to benchmark expenses and manage operations better.

Voluntary Health and Welfare organizations have been required to show expense allocation information as a statement or as part of the footnotes. Also, other nonprofits have been encouraged to show this information on the financial statements. However, after ASU 2016-14 (effective for fiscal years starting after Dec. 15, 2017), many more nonprofits are required to present this information. Some may display all in the Statements of Activities, while others may issue this statement instead, especially when they have more than one program.

✓ **The IRS requires a breakdown of functional expenses on Form 990, Part IX**

The Statement of Functional Expenses is a matrix-like report with headings for "Program Services" followed by "Supporting Services." Each of these headings usually involves a few columns. So, program services header includes columns for each major program. Similarly, the supporting services header shows administrative and fundraising expenses, although it could also contain a column for membership development and other functions that may be supportive in nature.

Additionally, the Statement of Functional Expenses shows natural categories, such as postage or rent as lines across the page. Each line is allocated among the functional columns. Thus, an expense, such as insurance, may have various numbers across, totaled on the last column.

Organizations should employ real, actual numbers in allocating expenses, not budget amounts. Computerized accounting systems help in this effort, although often worksheets are used to compile this report. Accountants start with the total numbers from the accounting system and then go line by line, classifying each expense by functional area, based on backup supporting documentation.

Supporting documents are likely to be time sheets, including electronic ones, invoices, etc. For example, nonprofits may allocate the utilities expense by using separate bills for each section, or they could allocate based on square footage of each area, assuming that is reasonable.

An example of a Statement of Functional Expenses follows.

Do-very-well-organization

Statement of Functional Expenses

6/30/20XX

	Program Services				Supporting Services		
	Animal Advocacy	Public Education	Primate Sanctuary	Bird Program	Administration	Fundraising	Total
Personnel	546,999	112,333	98,746	18,746	155,236	58,999	$ 991,059
Consultants	62,333	57,949			19,972	27,881	$ 168,135
Legal and accounting	15,866		3,368	1,699	35,229		$ 56,162
Postage and delivery	10,496	99,687	235		10,103	12,587	$ 133,108
Print/publications	2,630	58,666			8,327	2,396	$ 72,019
Feed			128,991				$ 128,991
Depreciation	8,991	2,580	3,669	1,588	8,999	877	$ 26,704
Contributions	6,333						$ 6,333
Advertising/Promotion	47,777	26,888			2,041	11,982	$ 88,688
Investment expenses	10,001	8,613	7,863		5,284	3,954	$ 35,715
Travel and conferences	20,336	2,553	2,995	1,036	1,702	95	$ 28,717
Telecommunications	11,764	4,246	5,804		1,868	679	$ 24,361
Utilities	5,688	2,781	9,984		3,660	967	$ 23,080
Insurance	4,271	1,280	13,017		2,204	1,355	$ 22,127
Equipment	1,039	742	3,373		686	371	$ 6,211
Veterinary	8,941		2,445	778			$ 12,164
Maintenance			2,719				$ 2,719
Other	6,999	2,333	875		566	2,699	$ 13,472
Total	$ 770,464	$ 380,651	$ 284,084	$ 23,847	$ 255,877	$ 124,842	$1,839,765

After ASU 2016-14, investment expenses are netted against investment income and not presented here, unless they're programmatic in nature. Also, all expenses should be shown by natural classification like rent, utilities and not "cost of goods sold," for example.

Note that the ASU 2016-14 requires a disclosure of the methods employed to allocate expenses in this schedule. A policy regarding this topic would be beneficial to keep allocations consistent.

✓ **The allocation of expenses for this schedule may be different from the cost allocation calculations and rates related to grant contracts.**

The program services section is spread into four columns because the organization has four major programs. In the example, expenses are up to par with expectations, with the programs area presenting the most charges, followed by administration, and fundraising.

As is the case with many nonprofits, the salaries/personnel line shows the most expenses. Accordingly, organizations should pay attention to this area to make sure it's accurate and reasonable. Many times employees move around, working in different areas, but the payroll coding in the system remains the same, charging salaries to the wrong project or grant. Management should review changes to payroll coding (or lack of changes) and time sheets often to make sure they're correct.

Some common problems with this functional statement are:

- Showing no fundraising expenses, but significant contribution revenues in other reports

- Classifying all expenses as programmatic

- Changing the allocation significantly on the tax returns

Liquidity

Liquidity refers to the cash situation of an organization. The FASB update ASU 2016-14 requires information about the liquidity of a nonprofit, including its ability to pay its bills one year after the date of the Statement of Position/Balance Sheet.

Liquidity must be shown in both qualitative and quantitative ways on the financial statements. Qualitative data determines how the organization uses its cash and includes classifying the Statement of Position items as current and non-current and setting up a policy for cash reserves that includes a time horizon.

Regarding quantitative information, organizations must show all liquid financial assets at year-end and any limitations in nature, by external forces, such as contracts, and internal forces, such as board restrictions. Also, disclosures should include details on lines of credit and any resource that helps with cash flows.

The idea is to show as much unrestricted cash as possible, including a nice cushion for unexpected expenditures. The standard is for an organization to have a reserve of about six months of expenses, but many are not focusing on that because of other concerns. So, management should focus a lot more in maintaining or targeting a certain amount for reserves each year. It's also important for the development department to focus on unrestricted funding sources and make sure any large gifts include a reasonable amount or percentage as unrestricted funds.

Analysis of Financial Statements

Management and donors often analyze financial statements to make informed decisions and identify trends. Each statement gives a different perspective on the financial health of an organization, such as how much cash is in the bank and the amount and type of expenses. However, it's essential to analyze each number as it relates to the others, to identify financial strengths and weaknesses of an organization.

Traditionally, people want to know how much an organization is spending in programs versus other areas. The more a nonprofit spends on programs, the better off it is. But there are other ways to analyze a nonprofit, discussed next.

Budget Analysis

Reviewing actual numbers versus budget is the first and most common way of analyzing financial statements. Managers review the numbers to see if any intervention is required. For example, if contributions revenue is significantly below budget, fundraising may need to be ramped up, or costs may need to be reduced.

When conducting this analysis, it's important to review monthly and year-to-day variances to evaluate the cumulative impact of the differences. The board of a nonprofit I worked at only looked at monthly and quarterly "Actual vs. Budget" reports, missing the mounting effect of smaller variances. It ended the year having to spend its reserve funds to pay the bills. Had the board evaluated cumulative differences, it may have increased fundraising earlier to avoid having to use reserves.

Review Past Financial Statements

A good way to evaluate financial statements is to look at past reports so that any significant changes can be identified and evaluated. As many reports include numbers for two consecutive years, this comparison is easy to do. But to get a better idea of trends over time, old statements should also be reviewed.

For example, if liabilities have doubled from one year to the next, the organization may be facing financial troubles, or there may be a strategic reason for the increase in liabilities, maybe related to an expansion of programs. Reviewing past information is a good way to analyze the financial numbers to see how the organization is performing as compared to other years.

Review Statements of Other Organizations

Many organizations post their financial statements and tax returns online that can be reviewed.

Financial information from other entities can be picked up from their websites, or from Guidestar.com, a website that displays tax returns for free. Be sure to review information from similar nonprofits in terms of size and niche. A small social work organization could be compared to other small nonprofit for the analysis to be useful. Many organizations post their financial statements and tax returns online that can be reviewed.

Publications geared towards this sector, such as "Nonprofits Times" or the "Journal of Philanthropy" often conduct research and publish financial information considered benchmarks

Focus on a Few Numbers

Looking at just one element, such as cash, doesn't give you enough information. However, if you see $100 as the cash balance, $200 in current receivables, and $8,000 in current liabilities, you're likely to be concerned about how the organization will pay its bills and be in business for long.

You may also compare the revenue section on the Statement of Activities with the cash and receivables on the Statement of Position. The revenues may be $20,000, but if you see $18,000 in receivables and $100 in cash, it's likely that most of the revenues consist of uncollected pledges, putting the organization at risk for weak cash flows.

Use Ratios

Businesses, including nonprofits, utilize ratios as quick ways to assess relationships between the financial numbers. By using ratios, one can compare financial data without reviewing the details, making it easy to compare the financial situation of several organizations. Instead of reviewing cash balances of two entities, users may look at current ratios, for instance, giving them additional information fast.

Banks are also interested in ratios, especially the debt and current ratios to assess the ability of businesses, including nonprofits, to pay their bills. Banks often mention ratios as part of loan covenants.

Some elements used in ratios, such as liabilities, should be monitored carefully. Increases in liabilities, for instance, are important. Such increases may be real debt or related to accounting updates (ASUs) that require certain transactions to be considered liabilities.

You can see some useful ratios next.

Name of Ratio	Formula	Goal
Current Ratio	Current Assets/Current Liabilities	Measure the ability of an organization to pay its current debt
Debt Ratio	Total Liabilities/Total Unrestricted Net Assets	Assess unrestricted net assets' ability to pay bills, loans, and the existence of any "cushion" leftover
Administration Cost Ratio	Total Fundraising+ General and Admin. Expense/Total Expenses	Common ratio to assess how certain expenses are allocated
Fundraising Efficiency	Contributed Income/Fundraising Expenses	Average amount of contributions raised from a dollar spent on fundraising

Summary

Nonprofits release official financial statements, such as the Statement of Position, Statement of Activities, and Statement of Cash Flows. Additionally, the organizations need to show expenses by function and nature, mostly done by preparing the Statement of Functional Expenses, showing costs in a matrix-like format.

ASU 2016-14 made changes to the financial statements, decreasing the number of net assets required and adding more disclosures to the official financial statements.

Analysis of these financial statements can provide information about the ability of a nonprofit to pay its bills, grow, and remain in business. A typical analysis is the actual vs. budgets report, but other tools, such as ratios and reviews of other nonprofits' financial reports could also be employed.

8 - Taxation

"The hardest thing to understand in the world is the income tax."

Albert Einstein

It can be a surprise to know that nonprofit organizations file tax returns, even though they're tax-exempt. Indeed, many organizations file information returns with several also paying federal, state, or local taxes. This chapter focuses on the federal reporting requirements.

The IRS, the primary U.S. tax agency, provides guidelines for nonprofit tax returns, which are quite detailed, including not only numbers, but also descriptions of mission statements, programs, and other pertinent information. The IRS website, www.irs.gov, offers both the tax forms and instructions for current and past years that can be downloaded or printed out.

Note that these tax returns have changed significantly since 2008. Before 2008, the IRS required less information overall about the organization. The earlier version had fewer schedules and no questions related to internal controls and other issues, as it's now the case.

Usually, organizations must file one or more of these tax returns annually, by the 15th day of the fifth month after the closing of the year:

- 990: *Return of Organization Exempt from Income Tax*- Regular tax return for nonprofits
- 990-EZ: *Short Form Return of Organization Exempt from Income Tax*- Summarized version of the tax return for smaller organizations
- 990-N: *e-Postcard*- Basic information for small nonprofits
- 990-T: *Exempt Organization Business Income Tax Return* - For taxable transactions incurred

Of all the tax forms, the 990-N is the newest, available for filing online only at the IRS website, www.irs.gov. This online form requests basic information about an organization, such as name, federal ID, and address.

✓ **Extensions of time to file returns are available.**

With all these options, what form should a nonprofit choose? Organizations decide which form to fill out based on gross receipts and assets.

As the threshold for filing changes often, be sure to check the IRS website before submitting the tax form. A nonprofit may fill out one form one year, but may be required to file another one the following year. See the IRS detailed guideline for filing next.

For year 2016:

Gross receipts normally ≤ $50,000 Note: Organizations eligible to file the *e-Postcard* may choose to file a full return	990-N
Gross receipts < $200,000, and Total assets < $500,000	990-EZ or 990
Gross receipts ≥ $200,000, or Total assets ≥ $500,000	990

The 990 is quite comprehensive, involving financial and other data, such as the mission statement, programs information, number of volunteers, and disclosure of certain policies and procedures. The IRS wants to have an overall idea about the organization, not just financial data.

The tax return is made up of the core pages of the 990 or 990-EZ and any other schedules. Form 990-Part IV shows a checklist for nonprofits to identify required schedules. Another section of the 990, Part VI, specifically relates to governance, management, and disclosures. It asks questions hinting at internal controls nonprofits should have, such as Item 13: "Did the organization have a whistleblower policy?"

✓ **If organizations don't file taxes for three consecutive years, their tax-exempt status is revoked - even small 990-N filers.**

Organizations should be concerned with losing their tax-exempt classification because this can create many problems. For example, donors will not be able to deduct their donations on their tax returns, and that may be unpleasant. Also, many grant applications are available online and will be rejected right away if the Employer ID Number doesn't match the IRS master list of tax-exempt organizations.

Note that the IRS may impose penalties if a nonprofit fails to file proper tax returns. According to the IRS website (www.irs.gov),

"Annual exempt organization return: Penalties for failure to file

If an organization fails to file a required return by the due date (including any extensions of time), it must pay a penalty of $20 a day for each day the return is late. The same penalty applies if the organization does not give all the information required on the return or does not give the correct information.

In general, the maximum penalty for any return is the lesser of $10,000 or 5 percent of the organization's gross receipts for the year. For an organization that has gross receipts of over $1 million for the year, the penalty is $100 a day up to a maximum of $50,000.

If the organization is subject to this penalty, the IRS may specify a date by which the return of correct information must be filed. If the return is not filed by that date, an individual within the organization who fails to comply may be charged a penalty of $10 a day The maximum penalty on all individuals for failures with respect to a return shall not exceed $5,000.

Please note: Automatic revocation occurs when an exempt organization that is required to file an annual return (e.g., Form 990, 990-EZ or 990-PF) or submit an annual electronic notice (Form 990-N, or e-Postcard) does not do so for three consecutive years. Under the law, the organization automatically loses its federal tax exemption."

To show "reasonable cause," the organization should include information indicating that management was not neglectful or careless, but that it had good reasons for not filing for an extension. Also, management must specify the steps it will take to avoid filing late again. A history of late filing doesn't bode well for the nonprofit. Forgetting to file isn't sufficient, although ignorance of the filing requirements by a 100 percent volunteer organization may be a reasonable cause.

Form 990

This form is usually filled out by the nonprofit's accounting manager or by outside auditors, as part of the audit engagement. One of the ideas is to make the board of directors more involved and responsible regarding the tax returns.

To illustrate, Part VI-Section B- Policies, line 11a asks, "Has the organization provided a complete copy of this Form 990 to all members of its governing body before filing the form?" Line 11b requires the nonprofit to describe the process of reviewing Form 990 in Schedule O.

Forms 990 and 990EZ are detailed, including a core and schedules to be used on an as-needed basis. Since the IRS requires the last three years of tax returns to be available to the public, these forms should be carefully prepared. People can request those directly from the organization, or through the IRS, the National Center for Charitable Statistics, Guide Star and other websites.

Note that nonprofits don't need to make public the names and addresses of contributors, although they are part of the tax return.

See next the core 990 pages along with explanations.

Form **990**	**Return of Organization Exempt From Income Tax**	OMB No. 1545-0047
	Under section 501(c), 527, or 4947(a)(1) of the Internal Revenue Code (except private foundations)	**2016**
Department of the Treasury Internal Revenue Service	► Do not enter social security numbers on this form as it may be made public. ► Information about Form 990 and its instructions is at *www.irs.gov/form990*.	**Open to Public Inspection**

A For the 2016 calendar year, or tax year beginning _____ , 2016, and ending _____ , 20 ____

B Check if applicable:	**C** Name of organization		**D** Employer identification number
☐ Address change	Doing business as		
☐ Name change	Number and street (or P.O. box if mail is not delivered to street address)	Room/suite	**E** Telephone number
☐ Initial return			
☐ Final return/terminated	City or town, state or province, country, and ZIP or foreign postal code		
☐ Amended return			**G** Gross receipts $
☐ Application pending	**F** Name and address of principal officer:		H(a) Is this a group return for subordinates? ☐ Yes ☐ No
			H(b) Are all subordinates included? ☐ Yes ☐ No
I Tax-exempt status: ☐ 501(c)(3) ☐ 501(c) ( ) ◄ (insert no.) ☐ 4947(a)(1) or ☐ 527			If "No," attach a list. (see instructions)
J Website: ►			H(c) Group exemption number ►
K Form of organization: ☐ Corporation ☐ Trust ☐ Association ☐ Other ►	**L** Year of formation:	**M** State of legal domicile:

Part I   Summary

Activities & Governance	1	Briefly describe the organization's mission or most significant activities: _____	
	2	Check this box ► ☐ if the organization discontinued its operations or disposed of more than 25% of its net assets.	
	3	Number of voting members of the governing body (Part VI, line 1a)	**3**
	4	Number of independent voting members of the governing body (Part VI, line 1b)	**4**
	5	Total number of individuals employed in calendar year 2016 (Part V, line 2a)	**5**
	6	Total number of volunteers (estimate if necessary)	**6**
	7a	Total unrelated business revenue from Part VIII, column (C), line 12	**7a**
	b	Net unrelated business taxable income from Form 990-T, line 34	**7b**

			Prior Year	Current Year
Revenue	8	Contributions and grants (Part VIII, line 1h)		
	9	Program service revenue (Part VIII, line 2g)		
	10	Investment income (Part VIII, column (A), lines 3, 4, and 7d)		
	11	Other revenue (Part VIII, column (A), lines 5, 6d, 8c, 9c, 10c, and 11e) . . .		
	12	Total revenue—add lines 8 through 11 (must equal Part VIII, column (A), line 12)		
Expenses	13	Grants and similar amounts paid (Part IX, column (A), lines 1–3)		
	14	Benefits paid to or for members (Part IX, column (A), line 4)		
	15	Salaries, other compensation, employee benefits (Part IX, column (A), lines 5–10)		
	16a	Professional fundraising fees (Part IX, column (A), line 11e)		
	b	Total fundraising expenses (Part IX, column (D), line 25) ► _____		
	17	Other expenses (Part IX, column (A), lines 11a–11d, 11f–24e)		
	18	Total expenses. Add lines 13–17 (must equal Part IX, column (A), line 25) . .		
	19	Revenue less expenses. Subtract line 18 from line 12		

			Beginning of Current Year	End of Year
Net Assets or Fund Balances	20	Total assets (Part X, line 16)		
	21	Total liabilities (Part X, line 26)		
	22	Net assets or fund balances. Subtract line 21 from line 20		

Part II   Signature Block

Under penalties of perjury, I declare that I have examined this return, including accompanying schedules and statements, and to the best of my knowledge and belief, it is true, correct, and complete. Declaration of preparer (other than officer) is based on all information of which preparer has any knowledge.

Sign Here	▶	Signature of officer		Date
	▶	Type or print name and title		

Paid Preparer Use Only	Print/Type preparer's name	Preparer's signature	Date	Check ☐ if self-employed	PTIN
	Firm's name ►			Firm's EIN ►	
	Firm's address ►			Phone no.	

May the IRS discuss this return with the preparer shown above? (see instructions) . . . . ☐ Yes ☐ No

For Paperwork Reduction Act Notice, see the separate instructions.   Cat. No. 11282Y   Form **990** (2016)

Form 990 (2016)   Page **2**

Part III	**Statement of Program Service Accomplishments**

Check if Schedule O contains a response or note to any line in this Part III . . . . ☐

1 Briefly describe the organization's mission:

_____

_____

_____

_____

2 Did the organization undertake any significant program services during the year which were not listed on the prior Form 990 or 990-EZ? . . . . ☐ **Yes** ☐ **No**

If "Yes," describe these new services on Schedule O.

3 Did the organization cease conducting, or make significant changes in how it conducts, any program services? . . . . ☐ **Yes** ☐ **No**

If "Yes," describe these changes on Schedule O.

4 Describe the organization's program service accomplishments for each of its three largest program services, as measured by expenses. Section 501(c)(3) and 501(c)(4) organizations are required to report the amount of grants and allocations to others, the total expenses, and revenue, if any, for each program service reported.

4a (Code: _____) (Expenses $ _____ including grants of $ _____) (Revenue $ _____)

_____

_____

_____

_____

_____

_____

_____

_____

_____

_____

4b (Code: _____) (Expenses $ _____ including grants of $ _____) (Revenue $ _____)

_____

_____

_____

_____

_____

_____

_____

_____

_____

_____

4c (Code: _____) (Expenses $ _____ including grants of $ _____) (Revenue $ _____)

_____

_____

_____

_____

_____

_____

_____

_____

_____

_____

_____

4d Other program services (Describe in Schedule O.)

(Expenses $ _____ including grants of $ _____) (Revenue $ _____)

4e Total program service expenses ▶ _____

Form **990** (2016)

Part IV Checklist of Required Schedules

		Yes	No
1	Is the organization described in section 501(c)(3) or 4947(a)(1) (other than a private foundation)? If "Yes," complete Schedule A	**1**	
2	Is the organization required to complete Schedule B, Schedule of Contributors (see instructions)?	**2**	
3	Did the organization engage in direct or indirect political campaign activities on behalf of or in opposition to candidates for public office? If "Yes," complete Schedule C, Part I	**3**	
4	**Section 501(c)(3) organizations.** Did the organization engage in lobbying activities, or have a section 501(h) election in effect during the tax year? If "Yes," complete Schedule C, Part II	**4**	
5	Is the organization a section 501(c)(4), 501(c)(5), or 501(c)(6) organization that receives membership dues, assessments, or similar amounts as defined in Revenue Procedure 98-19? If "Yes," complete Schedule C, Part III	**5**	
6	Did the organization maintain any donor advised funds or any similar funds or accounts for which donors have the right to provide advice on the distribution or investment of amounts in such funds or accounts? If "Yes," complete Schedule D, Part I	**6**	
7	Did the organization receive or hold a conservation easement, including easements to preserve open space, the environment, historic land areas, or historic structures? If "Yes," complete Schedule D, Part II	**7**	
8	Did the organization maintain collections of works of art, historical treasures, or other similar assets? If "Yes," complete Schedule D, Part III	**8**	
9	Did the organization report an amount in Part X, line 21, for escrow or custodial account liability, serve as a custodian for amounts not listed in Part X; or provide credit counseling, debt management, credit repair, or debt negotiation services? If "Yes," complete Schedule D, Part IV	**9**	
10	Did the organization, directly or through a related organization, hold assets in temporarily restricted endowments, permanent endowments, or quasi-endowments? If "Yes," complete Schedule D, Part V	**10**	
11	If the organization's answer to any of the following questions is "Yes," then complete Schedule D, Parts VI, VII, VIII, IX, or X as applicable.		
a	Did the organization report an amount for land, buildings, and equipment in Part X, line 10? If "Yes," complete Schedule D, Part VI	**11a**	
b	Did the organization report an amount for investments—other securities in Part X, line 12 that is 5% or more of its total assets reported in Part X, line 16? If "Yes," complete Schedule D, Part VII	**11b**	
c	Did the organization report an amount for investments—program related in Part X, line 13 that is 5% or more of its total assets reported in Part X, line 16? If "Yes," complete Schedule D, Part VIII	**11c**	
d	Did the organization report an amount for other assets in Part X, line 15 that is 5% or more of its total assets reported in Part X, line 16? If "Yes," complete Schedule D, Part IX	**11d**	
e	Did the organization report an amount for other liabilities in Part X, line 25? If "Yes," complete Schedule D, Part X	**11e**	
f	Did the organization's separate or consolidated financial statements for the tax year include a footnote that addresses the organization's liability for uncertain tax positions under FIN 48 (ASC 740)? If "Yes," complete Schedule D, Part X	**11f**	
12 a	Did the organization obtain separate, independent audited financial statements for the tax year? If "Yes," complete Schedule D, Parts XI and XII	**12a**	
b	Was the organization included in consolidated, independent audited financial statements for the tax year? If "Yes," and if the organization answered "No" to line 12a, then completing Schedule D, Parts XI and XII is optional	**12b**	
13	Is the organization a school described in section 170(b)(1)(A)(ii)? If "Yes," complete Schedule E	**13**	
14 a	Did the organization maintain an office, employees, or agents outside of the United States?	**14a**	
b	Did the organization have aggregate revenues or expenses of more than $10,000 from grantmaking, fundraising, business, investment, and program service activities outside the United States, or aggregate foreign investments valued at $100,000 or more? If "Yes," complete Schedule F, Parts I and IV	**14b**	
15	Did the organization report on Part IX, column (A), line 3, more than $5,000 of grants or other assistance to or for any foreign organization? If "Yes," complete Schedule F, Parts II and IV	**15**	
16	Did the organization report on Part IX, column (A), line 3, more than $5,000 of aggregate grants or other assistance to or for foreign individuals? If "Yes," complete Schedule F, Parts III and IV	**16**	
17	Did the organization report a total of more than $15,000 of expenses for professional fundraising services on Part IX, column (A), lines 6 and 11e? If "Yes," complete Schedule G, Part I (see instructions)	**17**	
18	Did the organization report more than $15,000 total of fundraising event gross income and contributions on Part VIII, lines 1c and 8a? If "Yes," complete Schedule G, Part II	**18**	
19	Did the organization report more than $15,000 of gross income from gaming activities on Part VIII, line 9a? If "Yes," complete Schedule G, Part III	**19**	

Form **990** (2016)

Part IV   Checklist of Required Schedules *(continued)*

			Yes	No
20 a	Did the organization operate one or more hospital facilities? *If "Yes," complete Schedule H*	20a		
b	If "Yes" to line 20a, did the organization attach a copy of its audited financial statements to this return? .	20b		
21	Did the organization report more than $5,000 of grants or other assistance to any domestic organization or domestic government on Part IX, column (A), line 1? *If "Yes," complete Schedule I, Parts I and II*	21		
22	Did the organization report more than $5,000 of grants or other assistance to or for domestic individuals on Part IX, column (A), line 2? *If "Yes," complete Schedule I, Parts I and III*	22		
23	Did the organization answer "Yes" to Part VII, Section A, line 3, 4, or 5 about compensation of the organization's current and former officers, directors, trustees, key employees, and highest compensated employees? *If "Yes," complete Schedule J*	23		
24a	Did the organization have a tax-exempt bond issue with an outstanding principal amount of more than $100,000 as of the last day of the year, that was issued after December 31, 2002? *If "Yes," answer lines 24b through 24d and complete Schedule K. If "No," go to line 25a*	24a		
b	Did the organization invest any proceeds of tax-exempt bonds beyond a temporary period exception? . .	24b		
c	Did the organization maintain an escrow account other than a refunding escrow at any time during the year to defease any tax-exempt bonds?	24c		
d	Did the organization act as an "on behalf of" issuer for bonds outstanding at any time during the year? . .	24d		
25a	**Section 501(c)(3), 501(c)(4), and 501(c)(29) organizations.** Did the organization engage in an excess benefit transaction with a disqualified person during the year? *If "Yes," complete Schedule L, Part I*	25a		
b	Is the organization aware that it engaged in an excess benefit transaction with a disqualified person in a prior year, and that the transaction has not been reported on any of the organization's prior Forms 990 or 990-EZ? *If "Yes," complete Schedule L, Part I*	25b		
26	Did the organization report any amount on Part X, line 5, 6, or 22 for receivables from or payables to any current or former officers, directors, trustees, key employees, highest compensated employees, or disqualified persons? *If "Yes," complete Schedule L, Part II*	26		
27	Did the organization provide a grant or other assistance to an officer, director, trustee, key employee, substantial contributor or employee thereof, a grant selection committee member, or to a 35% controlled entity or family member of any of these persons? *If "Yes," complete Schedule L, Part III*	27		
28	Was the organization a party to a business transaction with one of the following parties (see Schedule L, Part IV instructions for applicable filing thresholds, conditions, and exceptions):			
a	A current or former officer, director, trustee, or key employee? *If "Yes," complete Schedule L, Part IV* . .	28a		
b	A family member of a current or former officer, director, trustee, or key employee? *If "Yes," complete Schedule L, Part IV*	28b		
c	An entity of which a current or former officer, director, trustee, or key employee (or a family member thereof) was an officer, director, trustee, or direct or indirect owner? *If "Yes," complete Schedule L, Part IV* . . .	28c		
29	Did the organization receive more than $25,000 in non-cash contributions? *If "Yes," complete Schedule M*	29		
30	Did the organization receive contributions of art, historical treasures, or other similar assets, or qualified conservation contributions? *If "Yes," complete Schedule M*	30		
31	Did the organization liquidate, terminate, or dissolve and cease operations? *If "Yes," complete Schedule N, Part I*	31		
32	Did the organization sell, exchange, dispose of, or transfer more than 25% of its net assets? *If "Yes," complete Schedule N, Part II*	32		
33	Did the organization own 100% of an entity disregarded as separate from the organization under Regulations sections 301.7701-2 and 301.7701-3? *If "Yes," complete Schedule R, Part I*	33		
34	Was the organization related to any tax-exempt or taxable entity? *If "Yes," complete Schedule R, Part II, III, or IV, and Part V, line 1*	34		
35a	Did the organization have a controlled entity within the meaning of section 512(b)(13)?	35a		
b	If "Yes" to line 35a, did the organization receive any payment from or engage in any transaction with a controlled entity within the meaning of section 512(b)(13)? *If "Yes," complete Schedule R, Part V, line 2* . .	35b		
36	**Section 501(c)(3) organizations.** Did the organization make any transfers to an exempt non-charitable related organization? *If "Yes," complete Schedule R, Part V, line 2*	36		
37	Did the organization conduct more than 5% of its activities through an entity that is not a related organization and that is treated as a partnership for federal income tax purposes? *If "Yes," complete Schedule R, Part VI*	37		
38	Did the organization complete Schedule O and provide explanations in Schedule O for Part VI, lines 11b and 19? **Note.** All Form 990 filers are required to complete Schedule O.	38		

Form **990** (2016)

Part V Statements Regarding Other IRS Filings and Tax Compliance

Check if Schedule O contains a response or note to any line in this Part V . . . . ☐

			Yes	No
1a	Enter the number reported in Box 3 of Form 1096. Enter -0- if not applicable	1a		
b	Enter the number of Forms W-2G included in line 1a. Enter -0- if not applicable	1b		
c	Did the organization comply with backup withholding rules for reportable payments to vendors and reportable gaming (gambling) winnings to prize winners?		1c	
2a	Enter the number of employees reported on Form W-3, Transmittal of Wage and Tax Statements, filed for the calendar year ending with or within the year covered by this return	2a		
b	If at least one is reported on line 2a, did the organization file all required federal employment tax returns? .		2b	
	Note. If the sum of lines 1a and 2a is greater than 250, you may be required to e-file (see instructions) . .			
3a	Did the organization have unrelated business gross income of $1,000 or more during the year?		3a	
b	If "Yes," has it filed a Form 990-T for this year? If "No" to line 3b, provide an explanation in Schedule O. .		3b	
4a	At any time during the calendar year, did the organization have an interest in, or a signature or other authority over, a financial account in a foreign country (such as a bank account, securities account, or other financial account)?		4a	
b	If "Yes," enter the name of the foreign country: ▶ _____ See instructions for filing requirements for FinCEN Form 114, Report of Foreign Bank and Financial Accounts (FBAR).			
5a	Was the organization a party to a prohibited tax shelter transaction at any time during the tax year? . . .		5a	
b	Did any taxable party notify the organization that it was or is a party to a prohibited tax shelter transaction?		5b	
c	If "Yes" to line 5a or 5b, did the organization file Form 8886-T?		5c	
6a	Does the organization have annual gross receipts that are normally greater than $100,000, and did the organization solicit any contributions that were not tax deductible as charitable contributions?		6a	
b	If "Yes," did the organization include with every solicitation an express statement that such contributions or gifts were not tax deductible?		6b	
7	**Organizations that may receive deductible contributions under section 170(c).**			
a	Did the organization receive a payment in excess of $75 made partly as a contribution and partly for goods and services provided to the payor?		7a	
b	If "Yes," did the organization notify the donor of the value of the goods or services provided?		7b	
c	Did the organization sell, exchange, or otherwise dispose of tangible personal property for which it was required to file Form 8282?		7c	
d	If "Yes," indicate the number of Forms 8282 filed during the year	7d		
e	Did the organization receive any funds, directly or indirectly, to pay premiums on a personal benefit contract?		7e	
f	Did the organization, during the year, pay premiums, directly or indirectly, on a personal benefit contract? .		7f	
g	If the organization received a contribution of qualified intellectual property, did the organization file Form 8899 as required?		7g	
h	If the organization received a contribution of cars, boats, airplanes, or other vehicles, did the organization file a Form 1098-C?		7h	
8	**Sponsoring organizations maintaining donor advised funds.** Did a donor advised fund maintained by the sponsoring organization have excess business holdings at any time during the year?		8	
9	**Sponsoring organizations maintaining donor advised funds.**			
a	Did the sponsoring organization make any taxable distributions under section 4966?		9a	
b	Did the sponsoring organization make a distribution to a donor, donor advisor, or related person? . . .		9b	
10	**Section 501(c)(7) organizations.** Enter:			
a	Initiation fees and capital contributions included on Part VIII, line 12	10a		
b	Gross receipts, included on Form 990, Part VIII, line 12, for public use of club facilities .	10b		
11	**Section 501(c)(12) organizations.** Enter:			
a	Gross income from members or shareholders	11a		
b	Gross income from other sources (Do not net amounts due or paid to other sources against amounts due or received from them.)	11b		
12a	**Section 4947(a)(1) non-exempt charitable trusts.** Is the organization filing Form 990 in lieu of Form 1041?		12a	
b	If "Yes," enter the amount of tax-exempt interest received or accrued during the year . .	12b		
13	**Section 501(c)(29) qualified nonprofit health insurance issuers.**			
a	Is the organization licensed to issue qualified health plans in more than one state?		13a	
	Note. See the instructions for additional information the organization must report on Schedule O.			
b	Enter the amount of reserves the organization is required to maintain by the states in which the organization is licensed to issue qualified health plans	13b		
c	Enter the amount of reserves on hand	13c		
14a	Did the organization receive any payments for indoor tanning services during the tax year?		14a	
b	If "Yes," has it filed a Form 720 to report these payments? If "No," provide an explanation in Schedule O .		14b	

Form **990** (2018)

Form 990 (2016)   Page **6**

Part VI Governance, Management, and Disclosure *For each "Yes" response to lines 2 through 7b below, and for a "No" response to line 8a, 8b, or 10b below, describe the circumstances, processes, or changes in Schedule O. See instructions.*

Check if Schedule O contains a response or note to any line in this Part VI . . . . ☐

Section A. Governing Body and Management

			Yes	No
1a	Enter the number of voting members of the governing body at the end of the tax year . .	1a		
	If there are material differences in voting rights among members of the governing body, or if the governing body delegated broad authority to an executive committee or similar committee, explain in Schedule O.			
b	Enter the number of voting members included in line 1a, above, who are independent .	1b		
2	Did any officer, director, trustee, or key employee have a family relationship or a business relationship with any other officer, director, trustee, or key employee?	2		
3	Did the organization delegate control over management duties customarily performed by or under the direct supervision of officers, directors, or trustees, or key employees to a management company or other person? .	3		
4	Did the organization make any significant changes to its governing documents since the prior Form 990 was filed?	4		
5	Did the organization become aware during the year of a significant diversion of the organization's assets? .	5		
6	Did the organization have members or stockholders?	6		
7a	Did the organization have members, stockholders, or other persons who had the power to elect or appoint one or more members of the governing body?	7a		
b	Are any governance decisions of the organization reserved to (or subject to approval by) members, stockholders, or persons other than the governing body?	7b		
8	Did the organization contemporaneously document the meetings held or written actions undertaken during the year by the following:			
a	The governing body?	8a		
b	Each committee with authority to act on behalf of the governing body?	8b		
9	Is there any officer, director, trustee, or key employee listed in Part VII, Section A, who cannot be reached at the organization's mailing address? *If "Yes," provide the names and addresses in Schedule O*	9		

Section B. Policies *(This Section B requests information about policies not required by the Internal Revenue Code.)*

			Yes	No
10a	Did the organization have local chapters, branches, or affiliates?	10a		
b	If "Yes," did the organization have written policies and procedures governing the activities of such chapters, affiliates, and branches to ensure their operations are consistent with the organization's exempt purposes?	10b		
11a	Has the organization provided a complete copy of this Form 990 to all members of its governing body before filing the form?	11a		
b	Describe in Schedule O the process, if any, used by the organization to review this Form 990.			
12a	Did the organization have a written conflict of interest policy? *If "No," go to line 13*	12a		
b	Were officers, directors, or trustees, and key employees required to disclose annually interests that could give rise to conflicts?	12b		
c	Did the organization regularly and consistently monitor and enforce compliance with the policy? *If "Yes," describe in Schedule O how this was done*	12c		
13	Did the organization have a written whistleblower policy?	13		
14	Did the organization have a written document retention and destruction policy?	14		
15	Did the process for determining compensation of the following persons include a review and approval by independent persons, comparability data, and contemporaneous substantiation of the deliberation and decision?			
a	The organization's CEO, Executive Director, or top management official	15a		
b	Other officers or key employees of the organization	15b		
	If "Yes" to line 15a or 15b, describe the process in Schedule O (see instructions).			
16a	Did the organization invest in, contribute assets to, or participate in a joint venture or similar arrangement with a taxable entity during the year?	16a		
b	If "Yes," did the organization follow a written policy or procedure requiring the organization to evaluate its participation in joint venture arrangements under applicable federal tax law, and take steps to safeguard the organization's exempt status with respect to such arrangements?	16b		

Section C. Disclosure

17   List the states with which a copy of this Form 990 is required to be filed ▶

18   Section 6104 requires an organization to make its Forms 1023 (or 1024 if applicable), 990, and 990-T (Section 501(c)(3)s only) available for public inspection. Indicate how you made these available. Check all that apply.

☐ Own website   ☐ Another's website   ☐ Upon request   ☐ Other (explain in Schedule O)

19   Describe in Schedule O whether (and if so, how) the organization made its governing documents, conflict of interest policy, and financial statements available to the public during the tax year.

20   State the name, address, and telephone number of the person who possesses the organization's books and records: ▶

Form **990** (2016)

Form 990 (2016)   Page **7**

Part VII   **Compensation of Officers, Directors, Trustees, Key Employees, Highest Compensated Employees, and Independent Contractors**

Check if Schedule O contains a response or note to any line in this Part VII . . . . □

Section A. Officers, Directors, Trustees, Key Employees, and Highest Compensated Employees

1a Complete this table for all persons required to be listed. Report compensation for the calendar year ending with or within the organization's tax year.

• List all of the organization's **current** officers, directors, trustees (whether individuals or organizations), regardless of amount of compensation. Enter -0- in columns (D), (E), and (F) if no compensation was paid.

• List all of the organization's **current** key employees, if any. See instructions for definition of "key employee."

• List the organization's five **current** highest compensated employees (other than an officer, director, trustee, or key employee) who received reportable compensation (Box 5 of Form W-2 and/or Box 7 of Form 1099-MISC) of more than $100,000 from the organization and any related organizations.

• List all of the organization's **former** officers, key employees, and highest compensated employees who received more than $100,000 of reportable compensation from the organization and any related organizations.

• List all of the organization's **former directors or trustees** that received, in the capacity as a former director or trustee of the organization, more than $10,000 of reportable compensation from the organization and any related organizations.

List persons in the following order: individual trustees or directors; institutional trustees; officers; key employees; highest compensated employees; and former such persons.

□ Check this box if neither the organization nor any related organization compensated any current officer, director, or trustee.

(A) Name and Title	(B) Average hours per week (list any hours for related organizations below dotted line)	(C) Position (do not check more than one box, unless person is both an officer and a director/trustee)						(D) Reportable compensation from the organization (W-2/1099-MISC)	(E) Reportable compensation from related organizations (W-2/1099-MISC)	(F) Estimated amount of other compensation from the organization and related organizations
		Individual trustee or director	Institutional trustee	Officer	Key employee	Highest compensated employee	Former			
(1)										
(2)										
(3)										
(4)										
(5)										
(6)										
(7)										
(8)										
(9)										
(10)										
(11)										
(12)										
(13)										
(14)										

Form **990** (2016)

Form 990 (2016)   Page 8

Part VII Section A. Officers, Directors, Trustees, Key Employees, and Highest Compensated Employees *(continued)*

(A) Name and title	(B) Average hours per week (list any hours for related organizations below dotted line)	(C) Position (do not check more than one box, unless person is both an officer and a director/trustee)						(D) Reportable compensation from the organization (W-2/1099-MISC)	(E) Reportable compensation from related organizations (W-2/1099-MISC)	(F) Estimated amount of other compensation from the organization and related organizations
		Individual trustee or director	Institutional trustee	Officer	Key employee	Highest compensated employee	Former			
(15)										
(16)										
(17)										
(18)										
(19)										
(20)										
(21)										
(22)										
(23)										
(24)										
(25)										

1b Sub-total . . . . ▶

c Total from continuation sheets to Part VII, Section A . . . . . ▶

d Total (add lines 1b and 1c) . . . . ▶

2 Total number of individuals (including but not limited to those listed above) who received more than $100,000 of reportable compensation from the organization ▶

		Yes	No
3	Did the organization list any **former** officer, director, or trustee, key employee, or highest compensated employee on line 1a? *If "Yes," complete Schedule J for such individual* **3**		
4	For any individual listed on line 1a, is the sum of reportable compensation and other compensation from the organization and related organizations greater than $150,000? *If "Yes," complete Schedule J for such individual* **4**		
5	Did any person listed on line 1a receive or accrue compensation from any unrelated organization or individual for services rendered to the organization? *If "Yes," complete Schedule J for such person* **5**		

Section B. Independent Contractors

1 Complete this table for your five highest compensated independent contractors that received more than $100,000 of compensation from the organization. Report compensation for the calendar year ending with or within the organization's tax year.

(A) Name and business address	(B) Description of services	(C) Compensation

2 Total number of independent contractors (including but not limited to those listed above) who received more than $100,000 of compensation from the organization ▶

Form **990** (2016)

Part VIII	**Statement of Revenue**				

Check if Schedule O contains a response or note to any line in this Part VIII . . . . ☐

			(A) Total revenue	(B) Related or exempt function revenue	(C) Unrelated business revenue	(D) Revenue excluded from tax under sections 512-514
Contributions, Gifts, Grants and Other Similar Amounts	**1a**	Federated campaigns . . . **1a**				
	b	Membership dues **1b**				
	c	Fundraising events **1c**				
	d	Related organizations . . . **1d**				
	e	Government grants (contributions) **1e**				
	f	All other contributions, gifts, grants, and similar amounts not included above **1f**				
	g	Noncash contributions included in lines 1a-1f: $				
	h	**Total.** Add lines 1a–1f . . . . ▶				

				Business Code			
Program Service Revenue	**2a**	_____					
	b	_____					
	c	_____					
	d	_____					
	e	_____					
	f	All other program service revenue .					
	g	**Total.** Add lines 2a–2f . . . . ▶					

Other Revenue	**3**	Investment income (including dividends, interest, and other similar amounts) . . . . . . ▶				
	4	Income from investment of tax-exempt bond proceeds ▶				
	5	Royalties . . . . ▶				

			(i) Real	(ii) Personal				
	6a	Gross rents . .						
	b	Less: rental expenses						
	c	Rental income or (loss)						
	d	Net rental income or (loss) . . . . ▶						

			(i) Securities	(ii) Other				
	7a	Gross amount from sales of assets other than inventory						
	b	Less: cost or other basis and sales expenses .						
	c	Gain or (loss) . . .						
	d	Net gain or (loss) . . . . ▶						

	8a	Gross income from fundraising events (not including $ _____ of contributions reported on line 1c). See Part IV, line 18 . . . . . a				
	b	Less: direct expenses . . . . b				
	c	Net income or (loss) from fundraising events . ▶				
	9a	Gross income from gaming activities. See Part IV, line 19 . . . . . a				
	b	Less: direct expenses . . . . b				
	c	Net income or (loss) from gaming activities . . ▶				
	10a	Gross sales of inventory, less returns and allowances . . . a				
	b	Less: cost of goods sold . . . b				
	c	Net income or (loss) from sales of inventory . . ▶				

				Business Code			
		Miscellaneous Revenue					
	11a	_____					
	b	_____					
	c	_____					
	d	All other revenue					
	e	**Total.** Add lines 11a–11d . . . . . . ▶					
	12	**Total revenue.** See instructions. . . . . . ▶					

Part IX Statement of Functional Expenses

Section 501(c)(3) and 501(c)(4) organizations must complete all columns. All other organizations must complete column (A).

Check if Schedule O contains a response or note to any line in this Part IX . . . . ☐

Do not include amounts reported on lines 6b, 7b, 8b, 9b, and 10b of Part VIII.	(A) Total expenses	(B) Program service expenses	(C) Management and general expenses	(D) Fundraising expenses
1 Grants and other assistance to domestic organizations and domestic governments. See Part IV, line 21 . .				
2 Grants and other assistance to domestic individuals. See Part IV, line 22				
3 Grants and other assistance to foreign organizations, foreign governments, and foreign individuals. See Part IV, lines 15 and 16 . . .				
4 Benefits paid to or for members				
5 Compensation of current officers, directors, trustees, and key employees				
6 Compensation not included above, to disqualified persons (as defined under section 4958(f)(1)) and persons described in section 4958(c)(3)(B) . .				
7 Other salaries and wages				
8 Pension plan accruals and contributions (include section 401(k) and 403(b) employer contributions)				
9 Other employee benefits				
10 Payroll taxes				
11 Fees for services (non-employees):				
a Management				
b Legal				
c Accounting				
d Lobbying				
e Professional fundraising services. See Part IV, line 17				
f Investment management fees				
g Other. (If line 11g amount exceeds 10% of line 25, column (A) amount, list line 11g expenses on Schedule O.) . .				
12 Advertising and promotion				
13 Office expenses				
14 Information technology				
15 Royalties				
16 Occupancy				
17 Travel				
18 Payments of travel or entertainment expenses for any federal, state, or local public officials				
19 Conferences, conventions, and meetings .				
20 Interest				
21 Payments to affiliates				
22 Depreciation, depletion, and amortization				
23 Insurance				
24 Other expenses. Itemize expenses not covered above (List miscellaneous expenses in line 24e. If line 24e amount exceeds 10% of line 25, column (A) amount, list line 24e expenses on Schedule O.)				
a _____				
b _____				
c _____				
d _____				
e All other expenses				
25 **Total functional expenses.** Add lines 1 through 24e				
26 **Joint costs.** Complete this line only if the organization reported in column (B) joint costs from a combined educational campaign and fundraising solicitation. Check here ▶ ☐ if following SOP 98-2 (ASC 958-720)				

Form **990** (2016)

Part X Balance Sheet

Check if Schedule O contains a response or note to any line in this Part X . . . . □

			(A) Beginning of year		**(B)** End of year
Assets	1	Cash—non-interest-bearing		1	
	2	Savings and temporary cash investments		2	
	3	Pledges and grants receivable, net		3	
	4	Accounts receivable, net		4	
	5	Loans and other receivables from current and former officers, directors, trustees, key employees, and highest compensated employees. Complete Part II of Schedule L		5	
	6	Loans and other receivables from other disqualified persons (as defined under section 4958(f)(1)), persons described in section 4958(c)(3)(B), and contributing employers and sponsoring organizations of section 501(c)(9) voluntary employees' beneficiary organizations (see instructions). Complete Part II of Schedule L		6	
	7	Notes and loans receivable, net		7	
	8	Inventories for sale or use		8	
	9	Prepaid expenses and deferred charges		9	
	10a	Land, buildings, and equipment: cost or other basis. Complete Part VI of Schedule D **10a**			
	b	Less: accumulated depreciation **10b**		10c	
	11	Investments—publicly traded securities		11	
	12	Investments—other securities. See Part IV, line 11		12	
	13	Investments—program-related. See Part IV, line 11		13	
	14	Intangible assets		14	
	15	Other assets. See Part IV, line 11		15	
	16	**Total assets.** Add lines 1 through 15 (must equal line 34)		16	
Liabilities	17	Accounts payable and accrued expenses		17	
	18	Grants payable		18	
	19	Deferred revenue		19	
	20	Tax-exempt bond liabilities		20	
	21	Escrow or custodial account liability. Complete Part IV of Schedule D .		21	
	22	Loans and other payables to current and former officers, directors, trustees, key employees, highest compensated employees, and disqualified persons. Complete Part II of Schedule L		22	
	23	Secured mortgages and notes payable to unrelated third parties . .		23	
	24	Unsecured notes and loans payable to unrelated third parties . .		24	
	25	Other liabilities (including federal income tax, payables to related third parties, and other liabilities not included on lines 17-24). Complete Part X of Schedule D		25	
	26	**Total liabilities.** Add lines 17 through 25		26	
Net Assets or Fund Balances		Organizations that follow SFAS 117 (ASC 958), check here ▶ □ and complete lines 27 through 29, and lines 33 and 34.			
	27	Unrestricted net assets		27	
	28	Temporarily restricted net assets		28	
	29	Permanently restricted net assets		29	
		Organizations that do not follow SFAS 117 (ASC 958), check here ▶ □ and complete lines 30 through 34.			
	30	Capital stock or trust principal, or current funds		30	
	31	Paid-in or capital surplus, or land, building, or equipment fund . . .		31	
	32	Retained earnings, endowment, accumulated income, or other funds .		32	
	33	Total net assets or fund balances		33	
	34	Total liabilities and net assets/fund balances		34	

Form **990** (2016)

Form 990 (2016)   Page **12**

Part XI	**Reconciliation of Net Assets**		

Check if Schedule O contains a response or note to any line in this Part XI . . . . ☐

1	Total revenue (must equal Part VIII, column (A), line 12)	**1**	
2	Total expenses (must equal Part IX, column (A), line 25)	**2**	
3	Revenue less expenses. Subtract line 2 from line 1	**3**	
4	Net assets or fund balances at beginning of year (must equal Part X, line 33, column (A)) . . .	**4**	
5	Net unrealized gains (losses) on investments	**5**	
6	Donated services and use of facilities	**6**	
7	Investment expenses	**7**	
8	Prior period adjustments	**8**	
9	Other changes in net assets or fund balances (explain in Schedule O)	**9**	
10	Net assets or fund balances at end of year. Combine lines 3 through 9 (must equal Part X, line 33, column (B))	**10**	

Part XII	**Financial Statements and Reporting**		

Check if Schedule O contains a response or note to any line in this Part XII . . . . ☐

			Yes	No
1	Accounting method used to prepare the Form 990: ☐ Cash ☐ Accrual ☐ Other _____			
	If the organization changed its method of accounting from a prior year or checked "Other," explain in Schedule O.			
2a	Were the organization's financial statements compiled or reviewed by an independent accountant? . . .	**2a**		
	If "Yes," check a box below to indicate whether the financial statements for the year were compiled or reviewed on a separate basis, consolidated basis, or both:			
	☐ Separate basis ☐ Consolidated basis ☐ Both consolidated and separate basis			
b	Were the organization's financial statements audited by an independent accountant?	**2b**		
	If "Yes," check a box below to indicate whether the financial statements for the year were audited on a separate basis, consolidated basis, or both:			
	☐ Separate basis ☐ Consolidated basis ☐ Both consolidated and separate basis			
c	If "Yes" to line 2a or 2b, does the organization have a committee that assumes responsibility for oversight of the audit, review, or compilation of its financial statements and selection of an independent accountant?	**2c**		
	If the organization changed either its oversight process or selection process during the tax year, explain in Schedule O.			
3a	As a result of a federal award, was the organization required to undergo an audit or audits as set forth in the Single Audit Act and OMB Circular A-133?	**3a**		
b	If "Yes," did the organization undergo the required audit or audits? If the organization did not undergo the required audit or audits, explain why in Schedule O and describe any steps taken to undergo such audits.	**3b**		

Form **990** (2016)

The 990 core is divided into the following parts:

Part I- Summary Includes mission statement and number of employees and volunteers. Additionally, it presents totals of revenues and expenses by certain types, such as program services and professional fundraising expenditures. Totals of assets, liabilities, and net assets or "fund balances" are also required.

Part II- Signature Block This is the regular signature box.

Part III- Statement of Program Service Accomplishments Programs must be presented here with sufficient detail to link them to the mission statement, and to show the IRS and prospective donors that the program area is the heart of the organization.

Part IV- Checklist of Required Schedules Questionnaire must be answered to determine the schedules to be completed. Such schedules are detailed, enabling the IRS to evaluate any possible violation of the rules. Additionally, many nonprofits base their own policies and procedures on this schedule.

Part V- Statements Regarding Other IRS Filings and Tax Compliance Checklist presented with potential other compliance requirements not necessarily related to Form 990 itself, such as the number of W-2G filed.

Part VI- Governance, Management, and Disclosure Contains questions government and management policies while promoting transparency and accountability. Organizations want to respond "yes" to some questions, such as the one asking if the nonprofit has written policies and procedures for chapters to follow, ensuring consistency throughout the organization. Many nonprofits base their policies and procedures on these requirements.

Part VII- Compensation of Officers, Directors, Trustees, Key Employees, Highest Compensated Employees, and Independent Contractors This part reflects the IRS's concern with excessive pay and benefits. Part VI, lines 15 a and b directly relate to this area. If the organization answered "No" to either question and then shows salaries that are much higher than expected, the nonprofit may receive more scrutiny.

Part VIII- Statement of Revenue Sources of support are presented, including potentially taxable unrelated business income. This part can be analyzed carefully in case there is too much reliance on a sole source that is easily threatened in a weak economy. The expectation is for unrelated business revenue to be insignificant as compared with other income. Excess unrelated business revenue puts the organization at risk of losing its tax exemption (This statement excludes donations of services).

Part IX- Statement of Functional Expenses Presents the allocation of expenses among program, management, and fundraising expenses. The purpose is to demonstrate that the nonprofit has been using revenues properly, i.e., mostly in programs. Sometimes, fundraising or administrative expense numbers may seem excessive and need to be reviewed or justified, such as a new organization conducting fundraising to pay for programs not yet fully available (This statement excludes donations of services).

Part X- Balance Sheet Presents the Statement of Position data with more details, such as loans to officers, directors, and key employees. This part focuses on the liquidity and financial stability of a nonprofit.

Part XI- Reconciliation of Net Assets Shows a compilation of revenues, expenses, and other items, such as donated services, to prove that the total net assets number in Part X- Balance Sheet is correct according to the nonprofit's own financial reports.

Part XII- Financial Statements and Reporting This section requires details on the financial statements preparation, such as accounting methods and the work of an independent accountant. Moreover, this part covers audits and Single Audits, making organizations aware of these issues.

The 990 also includes salary information for highly paid executives and consultants. This isn't private information. Also, disclosures related to contractors and consultants aren't kept confidential. Because of this lack of privacy, some businesses decide not to apply for tax exemption.

Quite a few nonprofits use the 990s as marketing tools to display their programs and accomplishments, so it's common for the 990 to include extensive attachments, showing details of programs and the good they do in the community.

In case of address changes or changes in the identity of the person responsible for all tax issues, the nonprofit must file form 8822-B with the IRS.

Unrelated Business Income Tax

Nonprofits can have taxable income, known as Unrelated Business Taxable Income (UBTI). Organizations may owe taxes even if they only file the 990-N form. If an organization has UBTI of $1,000, it must submit 990-T Unrelated Business.

The government defines taxable income as income not substantially related to the organization's tax-exempt purposes or activities. The idea is to prevent nonprofit organizations from competing with for-profit firms unfairly. The tax due is known as Unrelated Business Income Tax (UBIT). Often, an activity generates unrelated business income if it meets three requirements:

1. It's a trade or business
2. It's regularly carried on, and
3. It's not substantially related to furthering the exempt purpose of the organization.

For example, an organization runs a pizza parlor selling pizza to the public. The nonprofit's mission and programs don't relate to the parlor's business. Also, the nonprofit pays employees to run the pizza place. All this information points to the pizza parlor generating unrelated business income that's taxable.

On the other hand, a humanitarian-service organization holds a bake sale. While the sale is unrelated to the mission, It's likely to be tax-exempt if not "regularly carried on." Nonprofit's activities are considered regularly carried on if they show a frequency, continuity, similarity to comparable commercial activities of for-profit businesses.

✓ **Form 990-T doesn't need to be available to the public.**

Some unrelated business activities may not be taxed. For instance, if an organization sells donated items, or if volunteers perform all the labor involved in the business, proceeds are exempt from taxes. Note that if the IRS notices too much UBTI, it may revoke the tax-exempt status, which can spell disaster for a nonprofit. To avoid this potential risk, most of the revenue must come from the public and mission-related programs. The percentage of business income should be minimal.

Nonprofits may also restructure their activities so that they're more aligned with the mission statement. So a travel program by itself may be unrelated, but if they add an instructor and a course component, and this program is more likely to be aligned with the mission, especially if it relates to an education-related nonprofit.

Note that an organization may even change its mission statement to fit the program. This requires filing amendments of the articles of incorporation with the state. Also, the IRS is notified with the annual 990. This may make sense to some nonprofits, but if done many times, it may become problematic with the IRS.

Other Tax Situations

Nonprofit organizations face various tax situations, besides income taxes. Many people assume that these organizations pay no taxes at all and that's not true. There are tax concerns with nonprofits' employees and others, such as those covered next.

Pension Plans

Nonprofits have the choice of offering two types of pension plans: the 403(b), a traditional annuity plan, and the 401(k), similar to the for-profit retirement plan. Under both plans, the employee contribution isn't taxed; but each plan has its own limits, laws, and regulations. Nonprofits need to file the proper documents with the government for those. A few organizations may offer the old-fashioned nonprofit-funded pension plan, but they are the exception. Proper filings need to be done for those as well.

Contractors

All nonprofits are required to comply with federal, state, and local laws and regulations regarding contractors. These organizations are required to file tax form 1099s related to vendors, just like any other business. Actually, 990-Part V, question 1a reads, "Enter the number reported in Box (3) of Form 1096, Annual Summary and Transmittal of U.S. Information Returns. Enter-0- if not applicable." (The form 1096 is the transmittal form for 1099s). So, the government is reminding nonprofits of this requirement.

Sales Tax

Nonprofits could owe sales, excise, or use taxes on fundraising and other revenue-generating events, depending on the state. Each state is different, and nonprofits must review the laws before any fundraising activity. California, for instance, collects taxes on certain auction items. Other states may not collect anything or may tax the entire gross revenue.

Some exemptions may need to be filed and approved before fundraising events; otherwise, the organization will owe sales tax as per state's laws.

Another Issue regarding sales tax is that nonprofits may need to pay sales tax on purchases, like any other business in California and other states. If vendors don't charge the organization such sales taxes, they may be liable for the taxes in case of a state audit, which may also trigger a state audit of the nonprofit. This can be costly.

Payroll

Payroll processes for most nonprofits are just like those of for-profits. The Treasury Inspector General for Tax Administration released a report in 2014 called, "Some Tax-Exempt Organizations Have Substantial Delinquent Payroll Taxes." In this report, twenty-five organizations received government payments over a three-year period of $148 million, including Medicare and Medicaid. Even though the organizations owned assets of more than $97 million, they didn't remit payroll and other taxes, including penalties. You can read this report at the government website: http://www.treasury.gov. So, it's clear that nonprofits must do better in this area.

Organizations should make sure that all deductions are taken, and all taxes are paid. Many times payroll-processing firms are misinformed about payroll responsibilities and process payroll with mistakes. Check with your state about specific state payroll considerations, including unemployment and disability insurance. Double check reports from payroll-processing companies to be sure all tax liabilities are covered.

An interesting topic for nonprofits is the issue of employees required to work as volunteers. This can be sticky. If anybody is required to volunteer, then it's not really volunteering, and employees could be eligible for overtime pay. If the organization doesn't pay up, it may be in trouble legally.

I suggest not requiring employees to volunteer, and if they do, pay them; in the case of exempt employees, give them paid time-off for the volunteering time.

The IRS and state governments don't allow nonprofits or for-profits to treat employees as independent contractors. Some of the rules to determine if someone is an employee or contractor are:

1. Behavioral: Does the company control or have the right to control what the worker does and how the worker does his or her job?
2. Financial: Are the business aspects of the worker's job controlled by the payer? (These include things like how the worker is paid, whether expenses are reimbursed, who provides tools/supplies, etc.).
3. Type of Relationship: Are there written contracts or employee-type benefits (i.e., pension plan, insurance, vacation pay, etc.)? Will the relationship continue and is the work performed a key aspect of the business?

The more positive responses, the more it's likely that the person is an employee, not a contractor. In the case of a dispute or government audit, the organization may be liable for taxes, interest, and penalties on employees classified incorrectly as contractors. This can be expensive.

Note that the IRS has enacted the Employment Taxes and Trust Fund Recovery Penalty (TFRP) "to encourage prompt payment of withheld income and employment taxes, including social security taxes, railroad retirement taxes, or collected excise taxes." The idea is to make one person responsible for payroll taxes.

Who Can Be Responsible for the TFRP?

"The TFRP may be assessed against any person who:

- Is responsible for collecting or paying withheld income and employment taxes, or for paying collected excise taxes, and

- Willfully fails to collect or pay them." (www.irs.gov)

Excise Tax

Excise tax relates to IRS "intermediate sanctions" that handle private inurement situations that don't warrant the loss of the tax exemption. The sanction, known as the excise tax, starts at 25 percent of the excess benefit and is imposed on the person who received the benefit. There is also a fine to the organization's manager involved in the transaction.

The IRS wants this tax to be paid promptly. "If the 25% tax is imposed and the excess benefit transaction isn't corrected within the taxable period, an additional excise tax equal to 200% of the excess benefit is imposed on any disqualified person involved." (www.irs.org)

An example of private inurement is if someone from a board of directors, or a relative, buys a house for $10 from the organization. The person was in a position of power and used it for his/her own benefit. The excise tax would be 25 percent of the value of the home, less the $10. The board member could also be liable for a fine of 10% of the excess benefit as an organization manager, unless he/she can prove that it was not willful and was due to reasonable cause.

Summary

Most tax-exempt organizations need to file 990 tax returns at the federal level, including the 990-N, the e-card filed online by small nonprofits. Forms 990 and 990-EZ request detailed information, such as mission statement, revenues and expenses, and program descriptions.

Unrelated business income requires nonprofits to file 990-T to report and pay taxes. The idea is to avoid giving nonprofits an unfair business advantage.

Other tax compliance issues are payroll, sales tax, and contractor identification and reporting. In some cases, excise taxes apply to certain individuals within the nonprofit organization.

9 - Internal Controls

"Quality is not an act. It's a habit."

Aristotle

Concepts of internal controls aren't new; they have existed for many years. If you can identify a risk, you can think up ways to minimize it with internal controls. The focus here is on checks and balances, responsibility, and accountability for financial information.

Internal control goals are to prevent losses and improve the reliability of the financial reporting. However, since every nonprofit is different, the control practices are likely to vary as well. To clarify and guide us on these issues, we have the Sarbanes and Oxley Act at the federal level, and state law requirements like the "Nonprofit Integrity Act of 2004" of California.

Also, the Committee of Sponsoring Organizations (COSO) of the Treadway Commission has promulgated a well-known integrated framework for firms to follow when considering internal controls in general.

The IRS is also interested in having nonprofits implement procedures to decrease fraud and losses while improving efficiencies. To this end, specific questions on the 990 tax return give clues about some controls expected, such as:

o   Does the organization have a written conflict of interest policy?

o   Are officers, directors, or trustees and key employees required to disclose annually interests that could give rise to conflicts?

o   Does the organization regularly and consistently monitor and enforce compliance with policy? If "Yes," describe in Schedule O how this is done.

o   Does the organization have a written whistleblower policy?

o   Does the organization have a written document-retention and destruction policy?

These questions are supposed to be answered in the affirmative, confirming these controls. At the very least, the nonprofits become aware of expected internal controls practices that should be seriously considered.

While many organizations base their checks and balances on tax returns, these aren't the only procedures available to help nonprofits monitor their daily operations. The idea is to examine a task, identify risks, and create preventive control procedures to eliminate or at least minimize such risks.

Internal controls don't need to be complicated or expensive. Small organizations can utilize standard processes, such as conducting monthly bank reconciliations to identify problem areas. Having someone from the board or the executive director take a look at bank transactions online can also be a useful procedure to identify many issues, including innocent errors and fraud.

Unfortunately, some nonprofits consider controls only after serious problems happen, such as significant losses due to errors or fraud. This type of attitude must change; management needs to be proactive about implementing proper procedures to avoid problems and not just react to issues as they happen.

Common Internal Control Practices

Some internal control practices are prevalent, helping in management and grant compliance. These controls are usually incorporated in the organizations' policies and procedures documentation, including specific activities to minimize errors and losses.

Not only is it important for nonprofits to implement these practices, but they must also maintain them to obtain full benefits. If procedures are followed only occasionally, the organization will still be at risk of fraud and errors. Therefore, as part of any internal control practice, there must be a mechanism to be sure they're indeed followed, such as checklists and management supervision.

Segregation of Duties

Segregation of duties involves the separation of certain activities to decrease errors and theft. The concept is to have more than one person participating in certain processes, so that if errors or fraud occurs during one step, the problem may be picked up on in another. In general, segregation of duties involves the separation of three functions:

- Custody of assets
- Authorization or approval of related transactions affecting those assets
- Recording or reporting of related transactions.

For example, the person who sends out invoices should not be involved in the receipt of money. If the same person were to handle these activities, he/she would be in the position to potentially pocket the money and fake-credit or delete the invoice from the system without anybody noticing the theft. Errors may also not be caught and fixed if one person does all the tasks, putting at risk the integrity of the information.

Following the same concept, only certain non-accounting people should initiate and approve discounts. Otherwise, anybody, including accounting personnel, may give unauthorized discounts to certain people and businesses.

✓ **A traditional feature of segregation of duties is for the person who processes bills and generates checks not to sign such checks.**

Managers not involved with accounting typically sign the checks. This may be a CFO if the nonprofit is large, and this person doesn't participate in the daily accounting activities. The payments are presented for signature along with backup documentation so that the signor can review it before signing the checks.

If segregation of duties isn't possible, which is often the case in smaller organizations, other controls can be in place to minimize the risks. For example, the treasurer could log in the bank website online and take a look at bank transactions once a week. Someone from the board may also review bank reconciliations and new vendor lists generated by the accounting system. Any odd vendor or amount can be identified, minimizing the risk of payments to fake vendors.

Computerized Systems

As software and computer costs have decreased, many nonprofits have relied on electronic systems that are quite sophisticated. Such systems not only help in calculations and reporting but also in the safekeeping of financial data. Usually, the information is backed up daily and can be retrieved without much effort. This is a significant advantage over paper-and-pencil systems, where pages can be lost and damaged easily. Unless copies were made of the paper ledgers, all information may be lost, causing delays and extra costs to replace the missing data manually. With a computerized system, some data may be lost, but it's usually a much more contained situation.

Electronic systems also help with security and internal controls because they require IDs and passwords. Managers can give rights to users, who can access only parts of the programs and not others. For instance, the accounts payable clerk should see only that area and not others, reducing the risk of errors and leaks of confidential information.

Advanced financial systems may allow for approvals on invoices online, saving time and streamlining the process. Sometimes such programs interface with a time sheet and/or customer service software, making it very efficient in capturing data without human errors.

Policies and Procedures (P&Ps)

Policies and procedures are used to control major decisions and behavior, so they take place within acceptable boundaries. P&Ps are usually based on internal control principles, mission statement, laws, and regulations. Many organizations use the tax returns questions to identify areas where P&Ps will be beneficial in improving internal controls.

Policies are general in nature, presenting guidelines based on the organization's mission and values. For example, a policy could be implemented to discontinue fundraising contact with any person who requested it orally or in writing. Based on this policy nonprofits may create various procedures to achieve this goal.

Procedures are specific, including steps, methods, and actions designed to implement a policy. It's common for a policy to include many procedures. Sometimes the procedures are so detailed they can be employed as a manual, while at other times, manuals are created from procedures, but contain more detailed information, such as print screens of some programs.

Together, the P&Ps unify the culture of an organization, simplifying decision making and setting the tone at the top. To this end, organizations often implement a number classification to structure the documentation. For example, P&Ps for the accounting department could be identified by the Section 300. If someone looks for a procedure related to assets, he/she will go to the Section 300, limiting confusion. Many nonprofits also include a table of contents to facilitate research and consulting of P&Ps.

Code of Conduct

A code of conduct supports the mission statement and its values. Such code presents proper practices and responsibilities of the nonprofit, including the board of directors and management. Typically, all employees and directors are required to sign off on this code, confirming having read it. Although not the same, the code of conduct is often called the code of ethics in many places.

The values of honesty and integrity are often mentioned along with unacceptable behaviors, such as sexual harassment. This document may mention inappropriate language in business communications and conduct, along with unsuitable pictures displays. It may comment on confidentiality, conflicts of interest, outside activities, and relationships with vendors and suppliers. It may also contain prohibitions against kickbacks and secret commissions. Many nonprofit organizations post their codes of conduct on their websites, such as the Weingart Center, at http://www.weingartfnd.org/Code-of-Ethics.

Specific Control Features

Traditionally, many nonprofits have certain controls to protect risky functions, such as cash transactions. However, there are some controls used in all sections of an organization, such as the requirement for all employees to take vacations (fraud and other problems are usually found when the employee is away).

Internal controls also help in catching and correcting innocent mistakes like reversing digits or duplicate vendors paid twice by mistake. For example, a nonprofit deposited a check for $100, but booked it on the accounting system as $1,000. With proper controls, this error can be identified and fixed

Note that not all controls are cumbersome or costly. They may be strange to those not used to the idea of controls to decrease risks, but they are worth it. You can review next some common risks and controls in various areas.

Cash- Receivables- Revenue

Cash isn't simply money, but also checks and credit card payments required to maintain the organization and pay its bills. Some key risks and controls with cash, receivables/revenue are discussed next.

Risk: Cash/checks can be lost or stolen.

Cash is a major risk for any nonprofit. As a control mechanism, two people should count any money before it's deposited to be sure the total is correct.

Also, organizations should acquire a safe preferably bolted to the wall or floor with the code known to limited personnel to safeguard cash, checks not yet deposited, and other valuables. Another control is to limit physical access to the area where money is received to just a few people.

Don't keep cash, checks, or credit card slips on a desk or in another unsafe place that is easily accessible. Thieves typically look for petty cash in drawers under desks.

As a control mechanism, nonprofits should use their websites to collect money as much as possible. Also, they could implement a policy indicating that no cash over a certain amount would be accepted to minimize the risk of losses. If money is received, it must be deposited promptly in the bank after the count by two separate individuals to confirm the amount of cash.

A nonprofit I know lost over $12,000 in cash brought to the premises. Somehow the money never made it to the bank, and it was unclear what happened or who was responsible for the loss. Soon after that, the organization decided not to accept any hard cash over $100 from anybody.

A traditional cash control is for nonprofits to perform bank reconciliations, also known as cash reconciliations, every month to be sure all cash transactions have been accounted for correctly. Reconciliations can be deterrents to cash theft. If people are aware that cash is monitored and reconciled, they might think twice before trying to "borrow" money. Errors can be found as well by using reconciliations; for example, if the accounting records include a check for $30, but the bank shows that same check as $300, then there is an error to be fixed internally or at the bank's side, depending on the situation.

Another control is for people outside accounting to answer phone calls or emails regarding complaints about payments not showing up in invoices. The question would be-- where's the money these people sent in? The problem could be just an error or an unfortunate situation where money is stolen.

Risk: Unauthorized credits/bad debt write-offs can be applied to receivables.

This risk often goes together with the loss of cash. Someone may receive payment in full, but instead of booking it, the person steals part or the entire amount, giving a credit, or a write-off for the difference. This way nobody will complain.

Controls to avoid this problem include segregation of duties, where the person who is in charge of accounts receivable doesn't handle money received by the nonprofit. Another control would be that all write-offs and credits to be initiated and approved by individuals outside the accounts receivable section, such as the executive director or a development manager.

Risk: Numbers for cash, accounts receivable, and revenues could be wrong.

Managers can identify this problem by reviewing an "accounts receivable aging report," a summary of the receivable details, also known as a "subsidiary ledger." Total in this report should agree with the number shown in the financial statements. Many nonprofits' accountants run and print aging reports as part of their "closing" each accounting period.

Errors may happen for various reasons. Sometimes mistakes occur when entries bypass the donor/member individual account. Instead of applying a payment to each subsidiary account, the accountant may apply the amount directly to the general ledger, skipping a step. Other times, the individual donor record is correct, but because of a glitch, the system doesn't transfer to the general ledger. Controls for these problems involve monthly bank reconciliations along with comparisons between the numbers in the aging reports and the ones in the general ledger.

Sometimes errors happen because of duplicate invoices sent out. A control for this risk is to centralize the invoicing function in one place so that one report can be reviewed with an eye toward identification and correction of possible duplicate invoices. Fundraising departments may send out invoices outside the accounting system, while the accounting department also sends out its own bills, creating duplication and confusion. Better to let the accounting department only do the invoicing process since it's the area best equipped to deal with financial matters.

Another possibility is donor duplication in the system. This could happen because of different name spelling or other problems. The result is that people may receive multiple invoices from the organization, which can create confusion. Management should run donor reports looking for similarities in addresses or other commonalities that can point to duplication.

Accounts Payable- Expenses

Accounts payable is part of any business, including nonprofits. Not only bills need to be approved and paid, but in the nonprofit world, they also need to be coded by area, program, and grant, making the recognition of each expense quite complicated. Some key risks and controls with accounts payable-expenses are the following:

Risk: Unauthorized payments occur.

Managers should approve all invoices, even if the costs are budgeted to avoid unauthorized payments. Also, the accounting department staff must be skeptical of all bills received, paying them only when they're approved. This process can be streamlined by using a "hot list" for utilities and other regular bills that may be paid without authorization, provided they're reasonable when compared with past expenses. Managers should review such hot list frequently.

Payments to fake vendors can be minimized by a supervisor review of "change/add vendor" reports regularly, as these reports are available in many computer systems. The person signing the checks can also identify unauthorized payments if he/she takes a close look at the backup documentation.

Since banking is often done via the Internet these days, if payments are made online using the bank website, a control may be for the bank to send an email to the executive director immediately after each online payment transaction. Another control involving the bank is to require two authorizations on any wire transfers.

To detect unauthorized problems, someone separate from the accounting tasks could log in the bank website and review payments online regularly. Just knowing that someone will look at online transactions at least once a week can be a deterrent to fraud.

Risk: Checks are changed after signed.

A control in this area may be to use banks' pre-approved list services, where checks are paid only if the payee and the amount of the checks agree with the ones on the listing. This service prevents checks that may have been stolen or modified from being paid. For example, if a check is presented for payment for $1,000, but is listed as $100, the bank will not honor it and will call the nonprofit regarding the payment. Sometimes accounting makes mistakes and checks are indeed legally changed. In this case, the staff needs to notify the bank of the error. This service can be expensive but may be worthwhile.

Nonprofits must keep its check stock safe in a locked place. They should also protect voided checks by keeping them in a safe place along with backup documentation. Only a few accounting employees would have access to these items.

Another layer of control would be for someone separate from the accounting department logging in and reviewing payments online in the bank website regularly. This person is likely to identify odd vendors, amounts and to ask questions. Just knowing that someone is looking online may prevent people from trying something nefarious.

Note that bank reconciliations could pick up this issue, since the number on the accounting system will be different from the number on bank statements. However, this control may not be that useful because by the time reconciliations are done, the person may have deposited or cashed the check and is gone with the money.

Risk: Double-paying vendors.

Organizations can minimize this common problem by using a computerized system that doesn't allow for duplicate invoice numbers. Also, nonprofits should implement a policy of paying invoices only and not statements, which may be filed for information purposes.

A traditional control is for accounting staff to stamp the invoices "Paid" so they don't pay the same thing again. Paid invoices can be marked as such in the computerized accounting system, in case the invoices are scanned and kept in a virtual environment.

Another mechanism is for the controller or accounting manager to review the accounts payable master list of vendors monthly to identify double entries of vendors. For example, a company may be listed as Ammy's Plumbing and as Amy's Plumbing in the accounting system. A payment went out under Ammy's name. Now suppose the vendor calls, and the person looks up Amy's Plumbing, sees no payments, and generates another check under that name, creating a duplicate check for the same vendor. An easy situation to be in.

Risk: Losing bills and paying late fees.

To prevent this problem, accounting staff should receive all bills and stamp them with the date received. It's common for vendors to send invoices to specific people, which may be a problem since sometimes bills are put in a drawer and forgotten until weeks later, which may result in late fees and bad reputation. Bills and invoices must be forwarded to accounting right away. Some organizations have special inter-office envelopes specific for this purpose.

Note that some bills may be paid late because they were emailed or snail-mailed to certain people who may be away or no longer working for the organization. These vendors must be identified and contacted with an updated contact email address.

Risk: Becoming a victim of scams.

Be aware of scam artists focusing on nonprofits. I witnessed a fraud involving printer cartridges. The deal was to mail out bad cartridges, and then send a bill for payment. Nobody really ordered the cartridges, but the scammer had a name of someone in the administration who supposedly ordered the items. In this case, the person had left the nonprofit many months before and could not have ordered anything. The sale was also not authorized by any managers, who knew nothing about the deal. The point is that nonprofits must have a reliable authorization control system to be able to avoid fraud like this.

✓ **Visit http://www.FTC.gov frequently, looking out for scams.**

Another known fraud is someone stealing a credit card, making a large donation online, and then requesting a refund on another card or a check for the money he/she supposedly donated. By the time the organization notices the problem, it may be too late, and the money is gone.

A control for the scam-type of fraud is for the accounting department staff and others to be on alert when they receive a bill, a mysterious delivery, or an odd request for reimbursement. I witnessed an accountant paying all bills received regardless of approvals because she was concerned about late payments. This isn't a good thing. Bills should be paid on time, but not blindly in a hurry.

Risk: Numbers for accounts payable and expenses could be wrong.

An issue with computerized systems is that the number showing up on financial reports may not be right. A manager can identify this problem by running an "accounts payable aging report" and comparing the total number on this report with the one on financial statements. They should agree. It doesn't make sense for a Statement of Position to show $300 in liabilities, while the payable aging report shows only $100; but it happens, pointing to mistakes.

Sometimes errors occur when entries bypass the individual vendor accounts. Other times, the individual vendor ledger is correct, but a glitch creates an error and the information isn't transferred properly.

Another issue is an input mistake when entering bills in the system. A good way to avoid this problem is to add up all the bills to be entered first, input the information in the system, run a system report on all bills entered. The total of the bills should match the total on the system report, and if not, accounting staff should be able to find and correct any errors.

Controls for accuracy problems also include bank reconciliations, where numbers on bank statements are compared with those in the accounting system. Management should review any discrepancies with a focus on checks that haven't shown up in the bank. These items may be lost and need to be voided and/or replaced.

Besides the risk/control issue, many states, such as California, require that "stale" (old) checks be forwarded to them once the check goes uncashed for too long. Nonprofits should contact their states for more information on this topic.

Payroll

Some organizations run on volunteers only, but many need employees to perform certain tasks. Since having employees is costly, it's no surprise that payroll is usually the biggest expense in the financial statements. Running payroll can be difficult, and while many organizations contract out outside payroll services, some prefer to process it in-house. Some key risks and controls with payroll are:

Risk: Time sheets could contain wrong information.

In many organizations receiving government funds, everyone files time sheets—even the president—to support charging grants "real" salaries rather than estimated/budgeted ones. Fortunately, many organizations use computerized timekeeping devices and time sheets that once implemented, reduce errors and confusion significantly.

A traditional internal control is for nonprofits to require supervisory approvals on time sheets (manual or electronic) to make sure hours and overtime are authorized. Auditors typically verify if the time

charged to a grant was allocated and authorized properly. If the auditor finds errors or no time sheets, or time sheets with no approvals, the scope of the audit is likely to increase, becoming more expensive.

Risk: Employees may be fictitious.

Each employee should file the proper paperwork with human resources and should visit the HR department personally. I know of a case where a program supervisor "hired" a relative part-time who was a "ghost employee." The nonprofit paid the "employee" for six months, while the supervisor cashed the paychecks.

It was only after a problem with the time sheet of this person (all fake) that the human resources manager got involved, and the fraud was discovered. So, it's crucial for HR to see and meet with all employees, including part-timers to be sure they're real and are actually working for the organization.

Risk: Unauthorized payroll changes or increases happen.

To make sure payroll records are correct, department managers should review and sign off payroll registers regarding their department at least once a quarter. Many department managers get the dollar amount of their department's payroll expenses through regular internal financial reporting, but not the details.

So, having managers verify payroll numbers, overtime, sick days, vacations, etc. is very helpful in keeping it all correct. If they see someone claiming overtime that the manager didn't approve, he or she can follow up on it.

Controllers or accounting managers should review payroll registers and change reports to make sure the persons running payroll aren't paying themselves unauthorized overtime or salary increases—a fraud I witnessed that could have been prevented had the controller taken a look at payroll reports regularly.

Risk: Paying terminated employees by mistake.

One issue I often see with payroll relates to nonprofits paying terminated employees because payroll staff didn't know about the terminations. . Once paid, it's tough to get the money back. So, it's important for human resources and managers to notify the payroll department when people quit or are let go. Staff may need to process final checks and update the payroll system.

Nonprofits may implement policies and procedures, including a checklist to follow when employees leave. Many details are involved, such as COBRA requirements that need to be handled correctly or the organization could be liable for fines.

Risk: Payroll information may leak.

Confidentiality is essential with payroll records. Nonprofits must keep all payroll-related documents, including time sheets, in safe, locked filing cabinets where only a few selected authorized personnel are allowed in. Similar security measures must be considered with access to the computerized payroll systems that should be very limited.

Nonprofits should hire people who are discreet and don't discuss confidential matters with others in the organization. They should avoid using email when mentioning any sensitive payroll information because the system may not be secure enough.

Information Systems

Many nonprofits keep confidential information on their computers, including sensitive data and details that can't be lost like donors and accounting information. So, security and controls involving information systems are necessary concerning the safety of servers, computers, printers, and the integrity of data.

A typical control of information systems is to have a disaster preparedness plan, which includes a recovery strategy for the nonprofit's functions. However, this isn't enough as issues with software, hardware, and cloud need consideration.

Software

Risks when dealing with software include unauthorized entry, loss of data, and confidentiality issues. Some internal control mechanisms to minimize these risks are:

- Use anti-vIrus and firewall programs to prevent malware from infiltrating the system.
- Do daily backups of all systems and keep the backed up file outside the premises.
- Require IDs and passwords on all systems.
- Acquire programs to identify and stop unauthorized entry using the Internet and other means.
- Require information system's authorization for program purchases to be sure the program is indeed needed and is compatible with existing software.
- Stop systems access once employees leave the organization.
- Include security to prevent information systems personnel access to passwords or confidential information.
- Create policies and procedures about computer usage and safety.

Hardware

The risks with hardware involve theft, maintenance, and obsolescence of the machines. Below are some controls to minimize these risks:

- Place all equipment, including servers and printers, in a safe location.
- Label all equipment with numbers and create a list of all equipment using the numbers and descriptions.
- Maintain this list, doing physical audits to identify equipment disappearances, losses and damages.
- Centralize maintenance services and schedule them regularly.
- Require IT management approval of all purchases, retirement or sales of hardware.
- Dispose of old computers carefully since they contain confidential information that may be recovered unless the nonprofit takes certain precautions.
- Dispose of old computers and peripherals complying with laws to avoid poisoning the environment and possible fines.

Using the Cloud

Many nonprofits have been using accounting and other programs "in the cloud." This means that organizations' management and staff access these computerized programs through the Internet, making the software very convenient since employees can access the system anywhere as long as they have proper online connections, login IDs, and passwords.

Organizations using old, unreliable equipment may benefit from the cloud since the data isn't saved locally. If the server or individual computers stop working, the information isn't lost and is still available.

However, we have risks associated with the cloud system. For example, the program may not be available online for long periods. So, before selecting a cloud system, check its reliability through Internet searches and word-of-mouth.

Once the organization decides to go online, management must trust the Internet provider to offer adequate security for the data, which may include donor information. Not surprisingly, data security of cloud systems is a major concern for both for-profit and nonprofit users.

Another issue with the cloud is the data transfer. If a nonprofit employs the cloud and then moves to another system, the existing data will need to be transferred to another program. The cloud provider should allow for such transfers and help the organization in this matter, but some may charge fees, so nonprofits must inquire about this issue early to avoid surprises later.

Summary

Nonprofits set up internal controls to minimize errors and losses in its operations. These procedures, evaluated by auditors, often involve segregation of duties.

Each place is different, but some common risks identified, such as cash theft, affect many organizations. Once risks are evaluated, controls can be established to minimize them. Monthly reconciliations, written management authorizations, and daily systems' backups are some of the controls employed to manage the risks.

Sheila Shanker

10 - Special Considerations

"Helping people doesn't have to be an unsound financial strategy."

Melinda Gates

Nonprofits have many issues that must be considered by managers and boards of directors, such as lease accounting, joint costs, budgeting, and human resources matters. While some of these issues also occur with for-profit businesses, they take on a different aspect when dealing with organizations whose main goal isn't to generate profits.

When dealing with special considerations for nonprofits, we must keep in mind that nonprofits focus on programs, the reason for the organizations to be in business. We must also bear in mind that these organizations rely on public assistance, such as government grants and donations and must use such resources wisely to be viable on the long-term basis.

Leases

Accounting for certain leases is changing for both nonprofits and regular businesses. We have two types of leases – operating and capital or finance lease. Operating leases are those paid as rent with no intent of ownership. A finance lease is like buying an asset and paying for it in installments.

Nonprofits account for an operating lease by recognizing expenses every period. It's the easiest one to book, as the same lease expense is recognized every month, usually for the same amount.

On the other hand, a capital lease recognizes an asset, a loan obligation, and interest. It also includes depreciation of the asset. Usually, after the first entry is made recognizing the asset and the loan obligation, all the entries are the same and can be set up on the accounting system to happen automatically. But that's not the case anymore for most nonprofits with fiscal years beginning after December 15, 2019, due to FASB ASU-2016-02 *Leases* update, which affects both for profit and nonprofit organizations alike.

Once this update, is implemented, we have different rules to identify leases and account for those that are over 12 months in length regardless if they're operating or capital. You can review this ASU at:

http://www.fasb.org/cs/ContentServer?pagename=FASB%2FDocument_C%2FDocumentPage&cid=1176167901010

The update keeps the operating and finance lease classifications, but there are major differences that affect the Statement of Position of lessees, which is the case with many organizations.

Both operating and finance leases now have two components that show up on the Statement of Position—the Right-of-Use Asset (ROU) and the lease liability. In many cases, both numbers will be the same, as the present value of lease payments. But if there are certain issues, such as purchase options, the amounts may differ.

Overall, the operating lease lessees recognize a total lease expense, while the lessees with finance leases recognize the amortization of the ROU and interest on the lease liability.

Nonprofits should be aware of the issues involved in this ASU since it requires complex calculations and different concepts that may be new to many.

Usually, organizations present financial statements for more than one year, so the financial data may need to be adjusted earlier than the time this ASU is supposed to be implemented. This is especially relevant to large nonprofits that may have foreign branches and several leases that need to be identified and analyzed to comply with this update.

So, start the conversation with your accounting department and outside CPA firm about this issue ASAP. Also, banks and other stakeholders must be notified of this change since it'll increase liabilities, affecting ratios and any covenants.

Joint Costs

Joint costs relate to ways to allocate expenses when a situation involves fundraising costs and costs in at least one more area, such as programs or administration. For example, a brochure could include elements of both fundraising and programs. The issue of joint costs is important because traditionally nonprofits prefer to classify most costs to programs, the least to fundraising, and this may not be a fair allocation.

Fundraising cost allocation issues were addressed by the AICPA Statement of Position 98-2, "Accounting for Costs of Activities of Not-for-Profit Organizations and State and Local Governmental Entities." The contents of this publication are now part of FASB ASC Subtopic 958-720, Not-for-Profit Entities—Other Expenses. This guideline provides a three-criterion frame of reference and requires that allocations be rational and systematic in their approach to joint costs. The nonprofit must comply with the standards, in this specific order, to assess the allocations:

1. Purpose of the event
2. Audience
3. Content

The FASB ASC mentions specific requirements within each of this criterion to determine whether costs are all allocated to fundraising or not. This can be tricky. If mailings contain a call for action, such as taking care of a health issue, promoting the nonprofit's mission, then the costs could pass the "purpose" test due to including a programmatic element. If the mailing provides information only, then the costs are fundraising only.

To pass the audience test, nonprofits can't send mailings to prior donors only or to primarily prior donors. If the organization does that, all the costs are classified as fundraising.

A nonprofit meets the criterion for content if the joint activity supports specific programs or G&A. For example, organizations may include financial statements to connect the mailing with G&A and qualify for joint costs.

✓ **Joint costs are mentioned on the 990 tax returns under Part IX- Statement of Functional Expenses.**

Interestingly, the standard doesn't specify the method for allocating costs other than that the process should be rational and systematic. Also, note that the Statement of Functional Expenses presents joint costs in detail after the allocation.

Budget

It's crucial for a nonprofit to implement an annual budget, an estimate of future revenues and expenses. Without a budget, an organization would be swimming in the dark with nothing to indicate if things are going according to plan or not. Many nonprofits submit their annual budgets to grantors as part of grant proposals to show that they have a doable plan and planning matter.

Also, the budget is a good internal control tool, helping to identify errors in accounting and even fraud. For example, if we see an unexpected variance on a line item, it could be because of an input or reporting mistake, or it could be a red flag for fraud.

Nonprofits create budgets based on history and information available at the time. Usually, it doesn't make sense to create a budget too early. I witnessed organizations creating budgets for board approval six months before the year-end, and that didn't work well. Too many things happened in six months, and the budget had to be totally redone a month before the new fiscal year. A budget created within the last two to three months of a fiscal year is often better and more realistic to be used in the following year.

Many organizations have a five-year plan with budget numbers attached to it. This plan is often revisited to be sure it still makes sense and to make adjustments as needed. Besides this long-term document, budgets are usually prepared for one fiscal year and are static throughout the year; however, many times, a "forecasted" amount is used to capture current information.

Some small organizations utilize prior year's revenues and expenses as budgets for the current year. This is better than no budget, but it doesn't give enough guidance for the future. An organization could start with prior years' revenues and expenses but should modify them to show a more realistic view of the nonprofit future. For instance, if supplies expense for the year was $1,000, and a couple of programs will be cut, then the budget for the next year could show an amount smaller than $1,000.

Often, nonprofits prepare estimated numbers based on accrual or cash methods. Some organizations do both budgets to manage cash during the year. The accrual basis budget recognizes revenues and expenses when they occur, not when they're paid. The cash basis recognizes transactions only when money exchanges hands. Both budget views are valuable, allowing management to see financial resources and flows from different perspectives.

Once approved by the board, the budget numbers are input into the accounting system for reports showing "actual versus budgeted" numbers throughout the year. Such reports are viewed by management to make sound decisions.

A major budget goal is to identify "holes" in the financial picture of a nonprofit. When all costs aren't covered 100 percent by grants, the organization must seek additional money through fundraising efforts. The best way to do this is to plan and know how much the nonprofit is supposed to raise for the year before it runs out of money.

Another budget goal is to avoid "double-dipping." The idea is that no expense can be funded by two or more sources. For example, an expense for $40 should be reimbursed by one source, not two. If the nonprofit submits the same expense twice, it will be reimbursed twice for one cost, "profiting" from the situation. A well-designed accounting system also helps in this case.

Many nonprofits implement a grant module to gather information on awards, including setting up separate budgets on each grant that, unlike the regular annual budget, can span multiple years, creating an extra layer of detail to help guide the organization.

Other Nonprofit Issues

Nonprofits possess some inherent issues that must be considered by management or donors. These are discussed next.

Tax Exemption

Once an organization receives the 501(c)(3) tax-exempt status, it needs to maintain it. According to the IRS, organizations can risk their tax-exempt status if they engage in certain transactions, such as:

- **Private benefit/inurement:** This issue is about private benefit versus public benefit. The exempt organization should serve the public, not a private individual. Examples are excessive salaries or transfers of property to insiders for less than fair market value.
- **Lobbying:** There are limitations to the amount of lobbying a 501(c)(3) can do. If it affects legislation and is substantial, lobbying can jeopardize the 501(c)(3) status of the organization.
- **Political campaign activity:** Organizations aren't to engage in any political campaign activity; they should not make donations or be involved in it.
- **Activities generating excessive unrelated business income:** Donations and other funds received are exempt from federal taxes, but certain activities not related to the organization's mission are taxed. Examples include sales commissions and membership list sales. When these become excessive, the IRS may question the organization's tax-exempt status.
- **Failure to file appropriate tax returns for three years:** Not filing tax returns is grounds for revocation of tax-exempt status.

The IRS can make mistakes, which may cost nonprofits their tax exemption. I know of one organization that lost its tax exemption a few months after getting it. There were no letters about it. The only sign of loss of tax exemption was that the organization was not on the IRS master database and could not file their annual taxes online. Many letters were sent out, and a few calls were made to the IRS to correct the situation without success. Finally, the Taxpayer Assistance Program fixed the problem. I highly recommend this program to any nonprofit experiencing unresolved issues with the IRS.

Pledges

Like for-profits, nonprofits utilize accounts receivable; however, unlike for-profits, the receivables are likely to be pledges and grants receivable. Nonprofits often can't collect on a few pledges, but there is no legal recourse. When there is legal recourse, it's usually not good for the organization's image. Also, pledges receivable aren't as safe and predictable as regular accounts receivable, especially long-term pledges. The risk of default may be high and should be monitored with phone calls and reminders to donors.

Note the strange situation of fake pledges. This is about someone making substantial promises for the publicity, but it was never real, causing embarrassment and loss of income to the organization.

Another issue with pledges happens when donors pay on pledges using stocks, but the value of the stock isn't high enough to cover the entire promise. In this situation, the pledge itself might be decreased, or the donor may need to pay for the difference. It can be tricky. This topic is covered in more detail on other chapters.

Human Resources

Hiring and keeping good employees is a challenge faced by most nonprofits. Many can't compete based on salary numbers. It also may be difficult to hire new employees because this sector may not be "sexy" enough.

Another issue is that some jobs may be funded one year and not the following year, creating instability and morale problems. Additionally, some nonprofits are located in dangerous neighborhoods and can't offer an attractive work environment, making the hiring and retention of employees more difficult.

So how can an organization attract and keep good employees? Some ideas are:

- Generous time-off policy
- Flexible working hours
- Possibility for employees to work from home
- Assistance with transportation
- Opportunities for professional development
- Lots of heartfelt public praise
- Possibility of student loan forgiveness when graduates work with certain nonprofits
- Referral program to other organizations if funds are cut, and employees are laid off
- Formal and informal mentoring programs
- Ability of lower level employees to share their ideas with executives

Nonprofit Resources

American Society of Association Executives:
http://www.asaecenter.org/

California Association of Nonprofits:
http://calnonprofits.org/

AICPA- Nonprofit Section:
http://www.aicpa.org/interestareas/notforprofit/Pages/default.aspx

National Council on Nonprofits:
https://www.councilofnonprofits.org/

Society for Nonprofits:
https://www.snpo.org/index.php

Sheila Shanker

__Summary__

Nonprofit organizations have their unique situations that should be considered, such as the concept of joint costs, where expenses may be allocated to fundraising & programs, or fundraising & administration. Another issue is the budget preparation and reporting. Changes in accounting for leases affect nonprofits as well.

There are a few matters inherent with the nonprofit sector, such as the possibility of losing tax exemption and the instability of pledge collections. Additionally, organizations must be aware of issues in attracting and keeping good employees to take the organization to the next level.

Conclusion

On a final note, dealing with nonprofits can be a challenge, but it can be gratifying as well. The nonprofit sector badly needs qualified people—those with not only good intentions and hearts, but also with sound technical skills, such as educated management, administrative, fundraising, and finance professionals. I hope that this book has inspired these professionals to join this sector.

I also hope this publication gives you a general roadmap to the nonprofits' issues and peculiarities. The similarities to the for-profit sector are many, but the twists may confuse many professionals, even those with many years of overall experience.

Usually, the confusion starts with the vocabulary. For example, after reading this text and understanding the term "temporarily restricted funds," you will be better equipped to have an informed discussion about financial matters.

I trust that this publication will help the overwhelmed finance professional or the new member of a board of directors to understand the industry better.

Best wishes in dealing with the nonprofit world!

Sheila Shanker

About the Author

Sheila Shanker is a CPA and MBA based in Culver City, sunny Southern California, where she lives with her husband and a demanding cat. She has been the Treasurer, Director of Finance and Controller for many organizations.

Sheila's long experience in the nonprofit sector has given her the inside track on what these organizations are really like, and what the finance professional and board member must know regarding accounting and financial reports. As a consultant, Sheila has helped many organizations in the finance and management areas.

Her book, "Nonprofit Finance: A Practical Guide," first edition, was nominated for the McAdam Book Award in 2016. Sheila's first book and course, "Guide to Nonprofits from the Trenches," was very well received by the nonprofit and accounting communities. She also created a book and online course about consulting that have received great reviews.

A prolific writer, Sheila has over 200 articles published in print and online, including articles for the "Nonprofit Times" and "Journal of Accountancy."

Sheila's background includes teaching online at the MBA program of the University of Liverpool (AACSB accredited). She also enjoys creating online books and conducting "live" classes and workshops. You can contact her through her website, www.webshanker.com.

Sheila Shanker

Glossary

Accounting	A systematic way of recording and summarizing financial transactions. It includes reporting and analysis.
Asset	Property owned that can be turned into cash.
Balance Sheet	A for-profit financial report that summarizes assets, liabilities, and equity.
Chart of Accounts	A list of all account numbers and their descriptions.
Cost Allocation Plan	A financial plan presented to a government agency to obtain funding and indirect cost rate for grants.
Determination Letter	A formal IRS letter proving that a nonprofit is indeed tax-exempt.
Direct Costs	Costs relating directly to a program, such as materials spent on an arts program only.
FASB	Financial Accounting Standards Board is a U.S. agency that establishes and communicates accounting principles employed in the U.S.
GAAP	Generally Accepted Accounting Principles is a framework of accounting standards and rules established by the accounting industry in the U.S.
General Ledger	List of all accounts and financial transactions of a business. It's the core of any accounting system.
Income Statement	A for-profit financial report summarizing revenues and expenses.
Indirect Costs	Costs relating indirectly to a program, such as insurance of a multipurpose building.
Joint Costs	Costs linked to activities involving fundraising and at least one more area of the organization.
Journal Entries	The mechanism to enter transactions into the accounting system, increasing or decreasing account balances.
Liability	Money or service owed to another party.

Net Asset	The element that accumulates and classifies transactions, similar to a fund.
Net Assets Released from Restrictions	The mechanism employed to transfer revenues from a restricted net asset to an unrestricted one.
Net Assets With Donor Restrictions	A net asset that combines the temporarily restricted net asset and permanently restricted net asset.
Net Assets Without Donor Restrictions	Same as unrestricted net asset.
Permanently Restricted Net Asset	Net asset that accumulates revenues permanently restricted by donors. Also known as endowment fund. Part of Net Assets With Donor Restrictions.
Statement of Activities	Nonprofit financial report summarizing revenues and expenses.
Statement of Cash Flows	Financial report of both for-profit and nonprofit organizations showing cash inflows and outflows.
Statement of Position	Nonprofit financial report summarizing assets, liabilities, and net assets.
Tax Form 990	Standard nonprofit IRS tax form.
Tax Form 990- EZ	IRS tax form for nonprofits, simpler than the 990.
Tax Form 990-N	IRS online tax form for small nonprofits, requesting basic information.
Tax Form 990-T	IRS tax form to report Unrelated Business Taxable Income.
Temporarily Restricted Net Asset	Net asset that accumulates donor-restricted revenues. Part of Net Assets With Donor Restrictions.
Unrestricted Net Asset	Net asset used for daily operations with no donor restrictions.

Index

Made in the USA
Coppell, TX
29 September 2022

83818737R00125